WHERE THE WATERS MEET

To dearest Marlene
with much love and
fondest memories of Bob
from David
November 2008

WHERE THE WATERS MEET

Convergence and Complementarity in Therapy and Theology

David Buckley

KARNAC

First published in 2008 by
Karnac Books Ltd
118 Finchley Road
London NW3 5HT

British Library Cataloguing in Publication Data

A.C.I.P. for this book is available from the British Library

ISBN-13: 978-1-85575-591-8

Edited, designed, and produced by HL Studios, Long Hanborough, Oxford

www.karnacbooks.com

Contents

Biblical quotations are taken from the New Revised
Standard Version

ACKNOWLEDGEMENTS

Writing this book has been both challenging and rewarding. I began writing it as an attempt to bring together some growing convictions around therapy and theology and was later encouraged to offer it for publication. I have no doubt that this would not have been realized without the help and encouragement of several people. There are many others, who are not mentioned here, who have had a profound influence for good on my life and who, down the years, have contributed to the thoughts and beliefs which I hold dear. I am made aware of many of these mentors, teachers, friends and befrienders, as I confine myself to acknowledging those who have had a special hand in enabling me to complete the manuscript. I would like to thank Christelle Yeyet-Jacquot of Karnac, who was my first contact with the publishers and whose friendly and careful handling of a naïve and rather nervous first-time author allayed many of my anxieties throughout the process. Lynne Matthews, a personal friend and psychotherapist has not only read versions of the manuscript with generous enthusiasm but her exceptional insight and passionate commitment to a psychodynamic approach has been an inspiration to me. Two friends whose academic ability far exceeds mine have given me invaluable and generous support throughout this last year, when the book has taken shape. Graham Patrick gave painstaking attention to the earliest drafts of my manuscript and without his perceptive comments and encouragement to complete the work I doubt whether it would have happened. Stephen Dawes has offered his friendship, scholarship and incisive mind to my cause frequently and I owe him a great debt of gratitude on all counts. My wife, Fran, has been my greatest encourager. She has borne with my many words and stumbling attempts to express myself and she has given me insights, sometimes without realizing it, which have either saved me from taking a wrong path or pointed me along a helpful one. Throughout the book I have used several examples from my Counselling work to bring alive important points. These examples have been disguised in order to protect confidentiality, without, I hope, destroying the point I wish to make.

ABOUT THE AUTHOR

David Buckley is a retired Methodist Minister and a psychodynamic counsellor and supervisor. He was born in Sheffield in 1943 and trained for ordained ministry in Birmingham, at Handsworth College and Queen's Ecumenical College.

In his work as a minister he has served in both rural and urban appointments throughout the UK. He has worked as a prison chaplain and for the last five years of his active ministry as the ecumenical chaplain to Kingston University, London. Throughout his ministry, he has maintained a keen interest in and commitment to ecumenism.

After gaining degrees in theology and biblical studies from London and Hull Universities, he developed a long-standing interest in psychology and counselling. During the 1990s he trained with the Westminster Pastoral Foundation, gaining several diplomas in psychodynamic counselling.

He now lives in Chipping Norton, where he has a private practice as a counsellor and supervisor. For the past four years he has worked as a counsellor for a large GP surgery.

INTRODUCTION

In July 2000, Lord George Carey, then the Archbishop of Canterbury, gave a keynote speech at a worldwide gathering of preachers.* In this speech Lord Carey criticised Western culture for being "beset by a reign of sin caused by an obsession with an unholy trinity of therapy, education and wealth." Aside from the naive and bewildering lumping together of the three offending quite disparate members of the "unholy trinity" the implication of this pronouncement is that therapy has become, for many people in the Western world (who presumably live under a "reign of sin"), a misguided and unhealthy alternative to religious faith. This view is itself misguided and unhealthy because whether or not people are turning to therapy as an alternative to religion, it fails to see that the two are not opposing forces but complementary channels of healing. The inspiration for writing this book has been to demonstrate that very point. Complementarity does not by any means preclude difference but by definition embraces it.

My aim in these pages is to reflect on the interplay between religion and psychology by comparing certain familiar doctrines, experiences and assumptions of Christian faith with the concepts and practices of a contemporary listening therapy – psychodynamic counselling. Clarification of terminology can be made later; for now I need to answer the more pertinent question of what might be the purpose of such reflection. To help answer that question I need to share some personal experience.

What has emerged as a book began as an attempt to write something for myself, about myself. The need was to express, in an ordered, integrated way, aspects of where my life's journey has brought me over the last decade or so, both personally and professionally.

I wanted to clarify and express thoughts and feelings which have grown within me and reshaped my theological and psychological perspectives. The reshaping of the two perspectives did not occur independently, as though they were two quite separate paths; often they intersected and at times became interwoven. This journey has not been spectacular. Indeed, in some ways, it seems to have been a natural path to follow. Yet paradoxically and subtly, it has been profoundly life-changing and has left me with passionate views on and around two areas of work which have engaged me over the last thirty five years and the two associated roles I have inhabited – as a Minister of Religion and as a Psychodynamic Counsellor.

What is private is not for sharing but we may choose to share what is personal if we feel something needs to be heard and if we think that sharing it may be of interest and help to others. What I feel needs to be said and heard, and what I shall attempt to articulate in these pages, is in part born out of frustration with and at times despair of, the Church – the same Church which embraced and nurtured me in younger days and through whose ministry I heard the faith proclaimed and saw it lived out. The same Church, through whose ministry I also ministered to others. My purpose, however, is not to launch an attack on the Church. To do so would, in any case, be an act of self-criticism, for its failings are often my failings.

It is certainly the case that in disclosing my purpose in writing, the Church (and by extension most forms of organized religion) will receive criticism but this "criticism" is frequently a sigh of sadness, or a cry of anguish that the Church all too often betrays what is precious about itself. It shoots itself in the foot and at times even manages to turn its message upside down and inside out, so that it ends up preaching and practising the very opposite of its true self.

Alongside my work as a Minister of Religion I was fortunate to be able to train, develop and practice as a counsellor in a role which was distinct from that of a cleric. The more I became involved in the world and work of counselling, the more I became aware of the strong, central themes which spoke implicitly yet profoundly about many essentials of Christian faith. I also became increasingly aware that these essentials are often the very things which the Church distorts, neglects, or petrifies within the cold grip of traditionalism, self-indulgence, insecurity, ignorance and fear.

The enthusiasm to share my thoughts about the similarities between religion and psychology may now become more apparent, if not yet entirely clear. To rely on religion (or Church tradition) alone as the primary, perhaps the only, "place" where we look for signs or verification of what the Church truly stands for and is entrusted to embody, leaves us in a strange and I would suggest, vulnerable position. Reliance on one source, of any kind, is a questionable base on which to build a solid belief, let alone commend it to others. Religion, like other spheres of life, has its particular jargon and terminology – "sin", "salvation", "Holy Spirit", "heaven", "hell", "God", "Jesus Christ". Such language carries coded messages because of the way in which it has been used, or misused, and consequently assumptions are made, or rather unconsciously accepted, as to what these words mean. Of course the rarefying and making exclusive of one expression of the truth is often aided and abetted by an organization's own desire to be special, exclusive and ultimately, controlling. This happens not only within religion but in most disciplines and movements. We might recognise it, for example, within politics, or even in "psychobabble".

I soon became aware that my attempt to pursue the theme of complementarity – as I found myself calling it – was a difficult, contentious and perhaps dangerous way to travel. As indicated above, jargon serves its own hidden agenda as well as having a legitimate role of interpretation. Attempting to see beyond the jargon by making comparisons and recognizing complementarity, can be seen and experienced as a threat and an attack. If the water I sail on is that of a reservoir, I can know its name and touch its boundaries. I can patrol and defend those boundaries from leakage within or intrusion without. But if the water I sail on is the open sea, it becomes less possible, sometimes impossible, to define whether the water is the sea, or one of its many rivers, estuaries or tributaries, for each flows into the other and partakes of the other. Yet the beauty and adventure of the open sea, or the rolling hills, far surpasses the limits of that which is manufactured . The latter may indeed have beauty and serve a necessary and vital purpose but – and this is the key difference – they are artificial, not in the sense of fake, or false but rather, temporary, or secondary. An artefact – if I may extend the analogy – may indeed be beautiful but it has its limitations. As my dictionary informs me, an artefact is "something made or given shape by man... anything man-made..." (Collins Concise Dictionary, 1982, p. 76).

Perhaps of further interest, another definition of artefact, used within cytology, "the detailed structure of a tissue as revealed by microscopic examination." (1982, p. 76), is: "a structure seen in dead tissue that is not normally present in the living tissue." (ibid, p. 76).

That which is living and life-giving may be carried, experienced, treasured and celebrated, within the artefacts of religion and Church but it cannot be confined to or shackled by those containers. If that is allowed to happen it becomes "dead tissue". To be "living tissue" religion, and church, need to be enthused and integrated with the truth common to all and to all creation. This discourse is intended to take us to the open sea where we can feel the swell- tide of truth beneath our bow.

The generous reader may acknowledge the value of my personal quest and even envy my enthusiasm for the journey, yet still want to ask what wider, global significance this has in the pursuit of truth, not least for their personal and corporate life. How do I, as the writer, justify making what is personal, public? To whom am I addressing my remarks and for what purpose? The street language for all of this might be, "Where am I coming from?" and – I would add - Where am I going? Answers to these questions are at least implicit in what has been written so far but need to be expressed more sharply and fully.

I am coming from a place of personal conviction that my faith tradition - the religion that has been built on the life of an ancient Jewish prophet named Jesus – is entrusted with a message and a way of life which is life-giving and vitally, crucially important for what it means to be a human being. I am not an evangelist and over the years I have become increasingly sceptical about almost everything which goes on in the name of evangelism. But it hurts me when I see the faith I believe to be live-giving, misunderstood, undervalued, or distorted. It hurts me when I do the same. It hurts me when I see folk in the Church, who silently cry out for a real interpretation of what faith means in the real world and are continually offered shallow, simplistic platitudes instead. It hurts me when I see, or hear of, those who turn away from faith, or never enter it, because they encounter dead rather than living tissue.

I am not an evangelist, but I find myself, without consciously seeking it, somewhere within the ancient Church practice of apologetics. The tradition of apologetics began by commending the (Christian) faith primarily to those beyond the Church communities, by giving a reasoned interpretation. Later the apologists also sought to defend the faith within the Church, against those whom they considered "unorthodox": "Their object was to gain a fair hearing for Christianity and to dispel popular slanders and misunderstandings, and to provide for this purpose some account of Christian belief and practice" (Cross, 1958, p. 71).

The Apologist, then and now, wants to say to those who wish to know and to listen that faith is believable. If I were pressed to give an overriding reason, which drives this book, I doubt that I could improve on the words of Paul Pruyser. Pruyser was a Dutch immigrant to the United States in 1948, Director of the Education Department of The Menninger Foundation, Senior Psychologist and authority on Psychology and Religion, who died in 1987. In the following quotation he is speaking of atonement theories, but his approach is consistent throughout:

> I have found that such a process of teaching and learning which articulates the psychological substrate of the atonement theories, is in itself a valuable stepping stone toward the acquisition of a new, contemporary, and more creative mode of symbol thinking. It may not only help revitalize many now antiquated and quaint, but in principle crucial Christian propositions, but also aid people in overcoming the crude, unnecessarily primitive and un-biblical supernaturalisms which abound in yesterday's and today's Christianity. [Pruyser, 1964, p. 111f]

Complementarity is, I believe, an important methodology and human experience, through which we can make sense of faith. None of this is about making faith easy to believe but it is about trying to prevent faith from being misunderstood, or presented in a way that is inaccessible, obscure or irrelevant. I have found that working with the complementarity between Christian belief and a psychodynamic way of understanding human behaviour is one way of making faith more understandable without compromising its depth of meaning. I cannot predict, or assume, who may find these pages interesting or helpful but I am certainly addressing those who are seeking to discover a faith which has integrity. That is to say, a way of believing and being human, alongside other human beings, which holds together, makes sense and has authenticity. I do this by giving particular examples of complementarity within psychology and religion. I shall also offer a more detailed description of what I mean by "complementarity" and why, as an approach or methodology, it is worthy of special note. However, before this can happen, some groundwork is necessary and I shall first give some consideration to the well established and on-going debate between religion and psychology. It will then be necessary to attempt a definition of what is being compared in the complementarity of "religion" and "psychology". I have already begun that task but a good deal more is required. The reader may not agree with my conclusions but I hope to make reasonably clear what I am comparing and why I draw those particular conclusions.

* The 3rd Annual Conference for Itinerant Preachers, Amsterdam, July 2000

PART I

Psychology and Religion

CHAPTER ONE

Differing approaches

There is a wealth of literature on the subject of psychology and religion and it is not my aim to offer anything approaching a review of this enormous field of study; to do so would require a book in itself. However, it will be helpful to indicate how this subject falls into several differing but overlapping categories.

Within this literature there are those who openly set out to demonstrate that religious belief is a colossal self-deception and who use psychology or psychoanalytical concepts and insights in an attempt to expose the fallacy of religion. Sigmund Freud, the commonly recognized father of psychoanalysis, is frequently quoted as the touchstone for this confrontation (sometimes referred to as the "warfare" model, reflecting the battle royal between science and religion). If Freud and his views are to be cast as the arch-enemy of religion we should at least recognise the nature of his opposition, especially since it is often misunderstood and misrepresented.

Although Freud is quoted – not least by many ardent adherents of religion – as the prime example of those who question the credibility of religion and find no usefulness for it in the lives of individuals or in society, he did in fact acknowledge the value of religion. By that I mean he recognized that it performed a function within society. Freud saw religion as an unconscious resistance to the intrusive and prohibitive presence of a human father, who unwittingly threatens to destroy the idyllic relationship of mother and child. Religion and particularly the concept of a heavenly father is, for Freud, our creation of a father-god, on whom we can be totally dependent. Although Freud regards this "projection" as a neurotic symptom, he argues that it has a usefulness in defending us against the realities of what he sees as our harsh existence. The following quotation demonstrates both Freud's attempt to expose religion as an "illusion", in the sense of a fallacy, and at the same time his understanding of religion as an illusion which has a usefulness for human beings facing the harsh realities of life. The italics are mine:

> Religions are remarkable compromise formations: they allow the human being to admit its extraordinary vulnerability and at the same time, to retain a sense of superiority in relation to the surrounding reality. The price for the compromise is the submission to an "illusion". Religious dogmas are not the results of experience or thinking, but they are refined fantasies, wish-fulfillments in response to the most basic needs of humankind. The strength of the illusion is therefore reciprocal to the strength of the need. The central religious fantasy, a Father-God, draws its material from the childhood experience of the human being: the child's helplessness creates the need for protection; this need motivates its love and expectations towards the father and forces it to suppress the hostility towards him insofar as he is also a rival in relation to the mother. But since the real father cannot remedy the fragility of human life, and since it does not end with childhood, a stronger and more powerful father is needed. In this way the father becomes idealized and projected into the image of God. The wish for protection, powered by the actually felt need, explains the strength of the religious belief. Although this is an inadequate response because it hides from the believer her or his real loneliness and the extent of the vulnerability, *Freud can come to understand religion in general as a useful neurotic and even psychotic symptom…It is a fantasy that makes life tolerable despite the hardships, and it even negates death as the final end of human life* (Braungardt, 1999).

All of this gives no comfort to the religious believer but it does give us an example of various ways in which psychology, or in Freud's case, psychoanalysis, is used as a critique of religion. There is a further point which makes it inappropriate to class Freud's confrontation with religion as "warfare". Freud enters into a dialogue with religion and several of his writings specifically address the subject. Towards the end of his life, he seemingly accepted that religion, neurotic symptom or not, was here to stay: "Life, as we find it, is too hard for us; it brings us too many pains, disappointments and impossible tasks. In order to bear it we cannot dispense with palliative measures" (Freud, 1930, p. 75).

The sting in the tale here, of course, is that by "palliative measures" Freud is indicating his view that religion is a form of drug. Nevertheless, dialogue is challenging and makes enlightenment possible. Believers who are prepared to listen may conclude that Freud's critique does reflect the way in which we can abuse religion to escape from reality. The religious person may wish to strongly challenge Freud's view by arguing that the purpose of religion is in fact to enable one to be utterly real by facing reality but which person of faith can deny the pitfall of using religion as an escape from reality? Where there is dialogue there are lessons to be learned; a point which keeps us anchored to the main purpose of this essay.

There are others who, unlike Freud, have a more favourable view of religion; who pursue a dialogue between religion and psychology which is informed and motivated by involvement and commitment to both faith and therapy. Brian Thorne, a leading "Person-Centred" therapist, has a short but powerful book subtitled *A Therapist's Meditations on the Passion of Jesus Christ* (Thorne, 1991), in which he brings psychological insight to stories of Jesus' last days. Thorne's book is offered as devotional reading but it is an outstanding example of how religious stories can be enhanced and given credibility through an imaginative, therapeutic interpretation. "Person-Centred" theory is a form of counselling pioneered by Carl Rogers (1902-1987), who developed his theory by placing emphasis on the efficacy of the counselling relationship and the client's right and ability to discover healing for themselves. These emphases are readily embraced within psychodynamic therapy models. I will return to Thorne's book later.

Jack Dominian, a well-known and widely-read Catholic author of pastoral and devotional books, who is also a psychiatrist, has attempted something similar to Thorne but not I think with the same success. His book, *One Like Us* (Dominian, 1998), is, as we might except from such an eminent figure, packed with valuable information and insights into the relationship between psychology and faith. Despite this, I do not find Dominian's approach helpful. His methodology for arriving at a psychological interpretation of Jesus is based on a direct comparison with the way he regards and responds to the stories of his patients. This methodology has the feeling of a circular argument.

As a psychiatrist I take the stories of the Christ of faith with utter seriousness. And this extends to their details. I accept them at face value and analyse them as I would any revelation made to me by my patients. I do so even if I am aware that certain details may owe their origin or their form to the catechetical concerns of the early Christian communities. [p. 11]

An example of Dominian's approach is his interpretation of the incident of the twelve year old Jesus' conversation with his parents in the temple (Luke 2,41-43):

"Every year his parents used to go to Jerusalem for the feast of the Passover. When he was twelve years old, they went up for the feast as usual. When the days of the feast were over and they set off home, the boy Jesus stayed behind in Jerusalem without his parents knowing it." [p. 68]

Dominian comments on this incident by imposing scarcely disguised psychodynamic concepts in order to create an apparently obvious, plausible link between the boy Jesus, the adult Jesus and the Christian Church of today. The most prominent of these concepts, that of *a secure base*, originates with John Bowlby (1907—1990) whose distinctive contribution to psychodynamic therapy I shall refer to later in Chapter 10. For the present it will suffice to say that the concept of *a secure base* emphasises how enormously important it is for a child to have an experience of security with a mother who keeps the child safe but also allows and encourages her child to venture, or to come and go. The following passage demonstrates how transparently Dominian uses the concept in the Biblical passage:

"This passage shows the secure self assurance of the boy Jesus, enabling him to stay behind and explore his environment, as well as showing his autonomy and his gentle rebuke to his mother: "Why were you looking for me? Did you not know that I must be in my Father's house?" But they did not understand what he meant" (Luke 2,49). Jesus' secure basis was internal, he carried it within himself. He in turn became the secure basis for his apostles and those who turned to him. In due course, he was to become the secure basis for his Church, which has survived to this very day." [*ibid.*, p. 63]

This "psychological interpretation" may well be interesting to and inspirational for a committed religious reader but I doubt whether it would commend itself to the non-believer.

Psychological models, concepts and insight can be used to explain religious experience, including the stories and miracles of sacred texts. Jung, for example, describes Paul's experience of blindness, on the Damascus Road, as "psychogenetic":

> Fanaticism is only found in individuals who are compensating secret doubts. The incident on the way to Damascus marks the moment when the unconscious complex of Christianity broke through into consciousness. Unable to conceive of himself as a Christian on account of his resistance to Christ, he became blind, and could only regain his sight through complete submission to Christianity. Psychogenetic blindness is, according to my experience, always due to unwillingness to see; that is, to understand and to realize something that is incompatible with the conscious attitude. Paul's unwillingness to see corresponds with his fanatical resistance to Christianity. [Jung, 1928, p. 257]

It is important to recognise that however unpalatable such an interpretation may be to some religious people, or whether Jung is anywhere near correct in his assessment, he is not wanting to dismiss or denigrate religious experience but to describe the unconscious, psychological processes that underlie such experiences. Jung's views on the psychology of religion are of particular interest to the religious person because of his own spiritual convictions. It is not my purpose to attempt a summary of Jung's views on the subject of psychology and religion but it is important to remember the colossal contribution he has made to the subject, especially in our understanding of the symbolic nature of Christian dogma. It is also the case that some of Jung's ideas have become household phrases and concepts; his work on "psychological types", particularly the definitions of *introvert* and *extrovert*, have been developed and used in various forms of personality-type testing. The most widely known of these is the "Type Indicator" developed by Isabel Briggs Myers and commonly referred to as "Myers-Briggs". (For those who wish to understand Myers-Briggs first hand, the clearest and most authoritative book to consult is *Gifts Differing* (Briggs Myers, 1980). I mention Myers-Briggs and its Jungian roots, in the context of my own agenda, because it is often used to understand the relationship between personality and spirituality; a typical contribution is Charles Keating's book *Who we are is how we pray* (Keating, 1987). Jung, therefore and the development and uses of his psychology, represents a further, differing approach to the relationship between psychology and religion.

There is another way in which the dialogue between religion and psychology has been pursued and presented which can be justifiably recognised as a tradition itself, within this field of study. It seeks to draw comparisons between various forms of developmental psychology – particularly those, like Freud's, which chart distinctive "stages" of human development. These stages are then likened and intrinsically linked to complementary stages of development in spiritual, religious and faith experiences. For those who have even a passing interest in the relationship of psychology and religion, probably the best known of these is J.W. Fowler's *Seven Stages of Faith* model (Fowler, 1981). The Stages, which are listed from 0 to 6, indicate a growth process which develops from a *primal faith*, through *intuitive-projective faith, mythic-literal faith, synthetic-conventional faith, individualise-reflective faith, conjunctive faith*, to its most refined and mature expression in *universalizing faith*. I have deliberately listed Fowler's terminology so that it can be clearly appreciated that the terminology which precedes the word "faith", represents the psychological dimensions of his theory. The psychological aspects of his psychology of belief model are informed by Piaget's work on the cognitive development of children, E. Erikson's Freudian-based model of the *Eight Ages of Man*, and the moral development model of the psychologist, L. Kohlberg.

For an overview and critical appraisal of the above models, Michael Jacob's *Living Illusions – A Psychology of Belief* (Jacobs, 1993), is outstanding. Not only does Jacobs offer a detailed description of Fowler's model, and acknowledge his indebtedness to it but he offers us a model which is broader and more flexible. Two of the critical features of Jacob's version are that, first, unlike Fowler's model, he uses the language of "faith" in a wider sense than "religion" and second, he releases the Stages from being age-specific, as in Fowler. This latter point is one of the great strengths of Jacob's approach. His appreciation of Fowler's stages model (and those of others) is tempered by awareness of its limitations, though I sense that any criticism is directed at how such models are interpreted and used, rather than the model itself :

> Although none of the models I have so far described *insists* on a rigidly linear scheme, there is nevertheless a temptation to link stages to ages,

and to see each stage as being complete in itself. Fowler indicates that the ages spanned by most of his Stages of faith have blurred edges. Transitional periods apart, it is important to remember that all these models involve dynamic movement, and that they are not to be understood as static. They have all been developed from the perspective of *psychodynamic* psychology. If stages have some value as signposts of human growth, when it comes to real psychological development, people pass into and out of (and back to as well as staying in) these various stages, depending upon external circumstances and upon their own internal responses to such eventualities. [p. 50]

and later, again speaking of the misuse of developmental models, Jacobs writes:

"There is also a temptation to use any of the categories or stages outlined in this chapter to caricature, stereotype or label others, whether as individuals or *en masse*, belonging to groups of which for one reason or another we are suspicious or critical." [p. 52]

Jacob's describes his own model as:

"...a possible psychology of belief, based on four themes: the first three of which I take from the stages of childhood which Freud identifies. I take the three terms "oral", "anal" and "genital" as being themselves metaphors: each one forms the matrix for a cluster of ideas, which helps make a collage of modes of belief. These modes may in some sense also be stages, although I have already expressed my caution about adopting too strict a linear model of "development". The technical terms and the symbols I collate point towards ways of understanding systems of belief." [p. 59]

Jacobs calls his fourth theme, *Letting Go*, which unlike the three, does not obviously stem from Freudian psychology.

I acknowledge here my own appreciation of Jacobs, not only for his amplified stages model and his caution in treating any model too rigidly or in a hierarchical fashion but for the whole scope of his book which deals admirably, and in an imaginative and positive way, with an understanding of faith as an illusion. I will freely draw upon Jacob's particular use of *illusion* later.

The developmental comparison models, as we might term them, have antecedents in the pioneering work of the study of religion and psychology. William James' *The Varieties of Religious*

Experience (James, 1902), is the classic example of this approach. James was a pioneering psychologist, theologian and philosopher, often described as belonging to the "school" of pragmatism This philosophical framework of pragmatism assumes a particular importance because James' approach to the psychology of religion became, either consciously or unconsciously, the touchstone for others. From a personal perspective it has been important to re-acquaint myself with pragmatism and to discover to my surprise that it feels like home ground – a natural place to be. Pragmatism therefore, from an objective-historical point of view as well as a subjective-personal one has an important place in the philosophical texture of this book.

Pragmatism is a philosophical methodology which begins with, and focuses on, practical consequences, rather than theoretical, or metaphysical propositions, in the search for understanding. James in no way discounts the need for ventures of faith. Indeed these ventures are absolutely necessary if faith is to be existentially realized, for we cannot discover whether something is true unless we experience it working in practice. James' own way of describing pragmatism is best heard first-hand. In his lecture *What Pragmatism Means* (in which "she" is James' circumlocution for "pragmatism") he concludes:

> In short, she widens the field of search for God. Rationalism sticks to logic and the empyrean. Empiricism sticks to the external senses. Pragmatism is willing to take anything, to follow either logic or the senses and to count the humblest and most personal experiences. She will count mystical experiences if they have practical consequences. She will take a God who lives in the very dirt of private fact – if that should seem a likely place to find him.

> Her only test of probable truth is what works best in the way of leading us, what fits every part of life best and combines with the collectivity of experience's demands, nothing being omitted. If theological ideas should do this, if the notion of God, in particular, should prove to do it, how could pragmatism possibly deny God's existence? She could see no meaning in treating as "not true" a notion that was pragmatically so successful. What other kind of truth could there be, for her, than all this agreement with concrete reality?

> In my last lecture I shall return again to the relations of pragmatism with religion. But you see already how democratic she is. Her manners

are as various and flexible, her resources as rich and endless, and her conclusions as friendly as those of mother nature. [James, 1904, p. 141]

In this first chapter I have given no more than a flavour of just some of the many ways in which psychology and religion interact and how others have viewed that interaction and formulated it. I have naturally been especially interested in those who work from a psychodynamic orientation but surprised to discover so little literature of this kind that is contemporary. Jacob's book has been a particular help and inspiration to me and from beyond the United Kingdom I have found the writings of Pruyser full of insight and courage. Within his specialist field of psychology and religion, Pruyser stands out as one of the most developed and authoritative figures since William James' ground-breaking contributions. He fits here also because he falls within the tradition of pragmatism and the descriptive method of James. He is in fact more akin to James than the other proponents of the developmental comparison models previously mentioned. Pruyser is able to avoid the limitations of a system or stages model. He thinks and writes more freely and directly, with a sense of immediacy and great passion, and like James his approach is more thematic than schematic. I will draw upon the writings of Pruyser and also Jacobs throughout, not simply as examples of differing ways of approaching the subject of religion and psychology but as important contributions along the lines of, though not identical with, my own particular approach. It is time now to state more clearly what that approach is.

CHAPTER TWO

Complementarity

The vast amount that has been written about religion and psychology in the past and the differing ways in which the subject has been explored might suggest that there is little need for anyone, let alone one who is essentially a practitioner rather than a professional academic, to write more. It could be that what appears to me to be a current dearth of material on the subject is an indication that little more needs to be said. My only justification for offering a further contribution to this debate is that the dearth may suggest the need for a significantly different emphasis; one that can make a meaningful contribution. The distinctive emphasis in what follows is the *methodology* used, and the way in which this methodology shapes the subject matter.

In the dialectic between religion and psychology, I want to suggest that alongside both the traditional discipline of the psychology *of* religion, and the psychological *interpretation* of biblical material or characters, there is a closely related but distinct area which focuses on the *complementarity* between the two. Psychology can be used as a tool, in an attempt to understand the phenomenon of religion. It can analyse, in a more or less scientific way, the psychological and emotional factors at work in a person's religious experience, or which lie within the great doctrines, myths and rituals of religion. Used in these ways, psychology either seeks to discredit religion by exposing it as a neurosis (dangerous and destructive or useful only as a coping mechanism and a self-deception, in face of the brutal reality of life) or to bring secular, psychological understanding to a sacred realm.

In the latter sense we have given some examples of how this has been done by comparing (often similar) developmental models of psychology with their suggested counterparts within religious and/ or faith experience. Although highly descriptive, these models have a specific framework, often related to faith-development "stages" and use psychological interpretation of faith phenomenon to make their point, rather than being led by a complementarity approach.

By now the reader may be justifiably enquiring where a complementarity approach to our subject differs from others. What in any case is meant in this context by the term "complementarity"? Frankly, I don't know where the word came from for me. "Complementarity" felt right; a suitable word to describe the approach I found myself using. It is, I understand, a term used in quantum physics and also in the field of economics but on both these fronts I plead ignorance. My greatest encouragement came from an old friend who was kind enough to read an early copy of the manuscript for this book. He mentioned having used such an approach (and the same terminology of "complementarity") in a university lecture – the lecture being on the subject of Science and Religion. The latter point is important in that "complementarity", rather like "existentialism", is an approach to a subject, a methodology, sometimes used unconsciously and intuitively, which does not dictate how the subject is framed but is led rather by what speaks to the enquirer of significant similarity. It is, to elucidate further, a methodology that requires a comparison and it is the comparison that drives and helps shape the outcome. The dictionary definition of "complementarity" is: "a situation in which two or more different things enhance each other or form a balanced whole" (*The Compact Oxford English Dictionary of Current English*, (2005)).

The use of this methodology does not mean that aspects of the "psychology of religion" mentioned in the previous chapter are not explored in this text; on the contrary, there will be constant overlapping and interaction but the driving force will be that which naturally presents itself as complementary.

Comparison is undoubtedly a component of complementarity but the latter has a wider meaning. it will also inevitably take on a meaning peculiar to the subject within these pages. In making a comparison, any thing may be compared to another thing but that which complements often has a paradoxical dimension. To take the simplest of examples: the colours blue and yellow may be compared, showing, for instance, that one is lighter than the other. If the comparison led to the comment that the two colours "go together" we could be talking of those colours complementing each other. The colours are decidedly different and yet each contains something which is intrinsically related to the other, something which allows them to "go together". Comparisons are made, even imposed; complementarity is discovered, or self-discloses. I detect something similar in Pruyser's approach when he speaks of a "perspectival... model". It is certainly not the same as complementarity but it has something of the same feel about it:

> I hope it is becoming clear that in the perspectival model which I uphold there is no limit on the *topics* that any team member can address. *The professional expertise represented by the team members is perspectival, not topical.*" Any perspective can potentially address anything, but does so in its own way, by the profession's special package of basic and applied sciences, skills, techniques, and language game. The perspectival view radically discards the older ontological and epistemological models that stage the disciplines as tightly bounded territories each representing a special kind of substance or neatly divide human nature into bodily, mental, and spiritual layers. Reality is far more fluid and holistic than these old models assume. [Pruyser, 1984, p. 96f]

I have stated above that comparison is a component of complementarity and I have indicated, as yet in only an elementary fashion, that the comparisons I shall be making lie within and between the two broad disciplines and experiences of psychology and religion. I have further defined these areas as being within psychodynamic therapy and certain doctrines or classic themes of Christian religion, experienced and understood from a personal theological perspective. None of this is intended to indicate cast iron containers and I have quite deliberately allowed myself to stray occasionally into, on the one hand, ideas beyond Christian religion and on the other, therapeutic approaches which originate beyond a psychodynamic therapy. I justify this fluidity because a complementarity approach allows for it, and calls for it; the hallmark of complementarity is that the boundaries of various disciplines and life experiences are not best understood as solid walls but as locks through which water can flow and travellers come and go.

In developing the theme of complementarity, it may be of help to know or to be reminded that at certain levels there always has been a close relationship between Christian faith and the world of counselling. This is apparent to anyone having the slightest interest in and experience of either. The founding figures of modern psychoanalysis were not avowedly religious, with the notable exception of Jung and even that claim requires careful qualification. It is, however, noteworthy that subsequent development of psychoanalysis (in the form of psychotherapy and counselling) owes a great deal not only to Freud, Melanie Klein, and their followers but to D. W. Winnicott, R. Fairbairn, J. Bowlby and many others, whose works do disclose an affinity with spirituality, if not religion. The establishment of training centres and voluntary agencies for counselling, which began in the 1960s and 1970s, owes a great deal to committed members of the Christian Church – of differing traditions – who saw the counselling relationship as a natural, though discrete expression of Christian caring. My own training agency, the Westminster Pastoral Foundation (which now has many affiliated centres), originated with an Anglican clergyman, Bill Kyle, and still attracts students from the ranks of regular church-goers.

What is the particular affiliation between Christian faith and therapy/counselling, beyond the obvious that both purport to share an interest in the care and wellbeing of individuals? This is where my line of enquiry comes face to face with a dilemma. Pressing the affiliation beyond the obvious may seem straightforward enough but it immediately leads into deep and often murky waters. Who says where complementarity is to be found, or more precisely, upon what comparisons it is based? The problem we face is the swirling waters of different views, mind-sets, or interpretations. This dilemma is more complex than the theological, ecclesiastical, or liturgical differences residing in denominations, or between the Roman Catholic and Protestant traditions. Those differences have proved to be challenging enough, as the battle-worn history of the ecumenical movement in the United Kingdom during the last century has shown. Even so it is not those differences in themselves which create the minefield which threatens to obliterate the signs of a real affiliation. It is rather the undercurrents of culture, folk religion, political bias and social outlook which, often unconsciously, drive and shape belief. Within these deep and murky waters there is also the considerably powerful area of personal and family "scripts" which are re-written over generations and the associated hurt which remains unexpressed – except that like all unexpressed, unresolved feeling, it takes the shape of distorted, even vengeful ideas and convictions and worse, ideas and attitudes which sometimes get "acted out" in personal relationships, church communities and social and political attitudes.

An example of the difficulties described above would be evident if, for example, the apparently non-contentious counselling catchphrase *unconditional positive regard* were to be discussed in the context of religious faith. The phrase is one of the "core conditions" of Person-Centred therapy already referred to, which describes the counsellor's required attitude towards a client, and by implication the required attitude for all wholesome relationships. Those who are familiar with this phrase, and those who are seeing it for the first time, may both recognise it as an ideal, uncontroversial example of complementarity between the religious life and the belief and attitude of the counsellor. This conclusion is strengthened by the awareness that Carl Rogers, the founder of Person-Centred therapy, is writing and practising from a position of religious faith. Even so, this factor would only make the complementarity compelling if the religious reader agrees with Rogers' interpretation of faith! There would be others who adhere to religion and profess faith, who would not warm to the phrase, or to its implications for how we behave towards others. Anyone who has belonged to a religious community, in which they have been thoroughly immersed for any length of time, will know of the dilemmas I allude to. I have heard genuinely caring, committed, church folk, including the ordained, declare that homosexual people who express their sexuality in relationship should be regarded in the same category as those who have committed murder. It is not uncommon, in my experience, to hear others refer to non-white people (and other minority groups) in a generalised and demeaning way, as well as using sweeping statements such as "them", when referring to those they dislike. I do not think that such language can be dismissed as simply "politically incorrect", or the language of a past generation, which however unfortunate is used innocently and without discriminatory intent. Sadly, the discriminatory intent is betrayed, all to often, in attitudes and behaviour. Political correctness and the use of non-sexist language is taken seriously by many contemporary Christians whilst others pour scorn on it and continue to be anachronistic and insensitive, let alone unchristian. The subject of crime and punishment can evoke, from some devout churchgoers, fierce outbursts of condemnation against criminal offenders, which takes no account of parental and social influences.

The dilemma described above is not of course peculiar to differences of opinion within religious communities; more testing and often destructive, is the differing attitudes and behaviour shown by those within the religious community to those beyond. How does the Church, often in the representative person of the priest, the vicar, or the minister, respond to the request, by a couple, to be married in the Church? I recall facing a pastoral dilemma some thirty years ago, when working as such a representative. I was asked by a couple, who I experienced as decent and delightful, whether I would conduct their marriage in Church. It was not a first marriage for either. Both had been divorced and had been living together as partners for several years. In my role as a minister of the Church I took seriously the responsibility to uphold the "standards" of the Church. Although my heart told me differently I kept to the "rules" and refused their request. I remind myself now that it was the 1970s. The Church had hardly begun to adjust to the changing patterns of social life, one of which was a radical reassessment of how couples responsibly manage their relationships. It was the "living together" in particular, which was still anathema to the Church, and indeed still is, whatever may be said and practised unofficially. For other traditions of Christianity, having been divorced would of itself been sufficient for the couple to be refused. Since that "pastoral dilemma" I have conducted many marriages for couples who were already living together, many of whom were divorced. The Church, on the whole, has moved on considerably in adjusting and responding positively in such circumstances. But there is still conflict as to whether *unconditional positive regard* can be applied in such circumstances. The compulsion to impose the Church's "standards" on those who have a differing life-style remains.

Only a few years ago, I had great difficulty in finding a Church in which to conduct a "marriage" service for a couple who had approached me in considerable distress. Neither had been married before, though they were an established couple living together. They had approached church after church, asking for help. Often the refusal was curt and cold. The "problem" was that they were both women. Although it took a while I eventually found a church that was happy to accommodate the couple's request and I conducted a Service of Blessing for them.

Unconditional positive regard may sound like a splendid summary of Christian faith in action but when the action is looked for, the Church is divided. Of course I am aware of the need for a serious debate about the difference between regarding someone unconditionally etc. and that of facilitating someone to do whatever they wish. The need for such a debate is precisely the point I am making; no one representing the Church can be excused from wrestling with the question of what constitutes a God-like and in the case of Christianity, a Christ-like response, in such circumstances. It is perhaps too often assumed by the religious that ecclesiastical "laws" are superior to the attitudes and life-styles of those who differ.

The picture I have painted, of conflicting attitudes within Church communities and of professing Christians towards those not explicitly committed to the Church, is not meant to imply that prejudice and insensitivity predominates. My experience of more than forty five years as a member of the Church, of which more than thirty have been as a practising ordained minister, is that such views represent a minority. It is, however, a sizeable and vocal minority, which should not be ignored. It would be quite misleading and inaccurate to suggest that these expressions of Christian faith go hand-in-hand with a particular theological outlook or stance. The picture is far more complex and a further examination would take us into the realm of a psychological examination and attempted interpretation, of the belief systems of individuals and the social, cultural and emotional factors involved. This is not the task I am pursuing. However, It is necessary to refer to the controversy, since whatever the reasons (hidden or otherwise) for the diametrically opposed views of committed church members, each person is entitled and should be encouraged, to make a judgement (without being judgmental) about the attitudes which are appropriate for someone who uses the name "Christian" and who belongs to the religion which bears that name.

In the last resort we have no alternative but to take responsibility for our own views, aware of our failures and susceptibility to hypocrisy, prejudice, self-indulgence and the damaging effects of unexamined, untreated inner conflicts. This we share with the whole of humanity. To be aware of these things is the first step; to increasingly rise above them and catch a vision of what stands to reason and rings true in the depths of our soul, is the most we can do – and the least.

I have acknowledged that using complementarity as a methodology is not without its problems. The comparisons that are inevitable within such an approach need to be defined and this will involve a careful balance between what is handed down – the tradition – and how an individual or school of thought interprets that tradition. What strikes me as convergence and complementary, in considering a comparison between an aspect of Christian doctrine and a tenet of psychodynamic therapy, may be seen by another as divergence and confliction.

CHAPTER THREE

Tributaries

B efore I attempt, in the second part of this book, to lay down my own perspectives of theology and therapy, there is a subject that I want to address. It requires attention at this point because it considerably informs and shapes those perspectives. It is a subject which of itself indicates a fascinating complementarity but it belongs here because it is an example of how a *third* discipline complements the other two. It is, so to speak, a tributary; a powerful tributary which over time has flowed into other waters and made its contribution. This tributary is the discipline of *Literary Criticism* and although for many generations it has had a kindred stream in the world of biblical studies, within what is commonly referred to as *Biblical Interpretation* or *Hermeneutics*, it has a life and tradition of its own, beyond religion. Margaret Davies helpfully points out how this similarity-come-difference can present itself as confusion. She refers to early (late 19th century) attempts by biblical scholars who "[reached] behind the texts to their sources, and the events which gave rise to them. (This type of scholarship has often been referred to as "literary criticism", but is more appropriately described as "source criticism"…)" (Davies, 1990, p. 402).

During the last quarter of a century some critical shifts in biblical interpretation have taken place, particularly about how passages of Scripture are approached, read and responded to. I will set this within a larger picture, beginning in the latter part of the nineteenth century. This will be highly condensed and inevitably sketchy. My aim however is not to say all that can be said about hermeneutics but to highlight the shifts which have encouraged and facilitated a play-full, creative interaction between psychodynamic psychology and religious stories and doctrines.

Those, like myself, who were theologically trained in the 1960s (and many who were trained before) approached the Bible armed with several disciplines. *Source criticism* seeks to understand the origins of texts that deal with the same subject matter but present or interpret it in differing sometimes conflicting ways, or the literary relationship between whole passages of the Bible in the form of narrative, parable, or story. Probably the best known example of *source criticism* has been the study of how the first three, "synoptic" (i.e. "can be seen together or alongside each other") gospels, relate, textually. *Form criticism* identifies literary styles common to ancient writing in order to help us better understand particular passages of scripture. *Redaction criticism* recognizes and takes into account the motives, purpose and theological perspective of the writer, or more likely the school of thought that produced a gospel, epistle, or story.

These methods of understanding the Bible often overlapped but their common factor was a critical investigation and appreciation of what was actually written in the original languages; where it came from, how it had been put together, and what it was intended to say. We sought, with these tools, to interpret a text – whether in the form of a saying or story – with an objective critique, locating it, as far as was possible, within its historical setting, its *sitz im leben* (life situation), or rather, its *several* historical settings) before attempting to re-interpret it for our contemporary situation. There was no room for romancing about the stories of Jesus, or using those stories merely as pegs on which to hang our latest idea. Jeremias' monumental work on the parables of Jesus is a good example of how painstaking and scholarly interpretation could be exciting and bring alive the biblical scene. A specific example of this is the interpretation of how the parable of The Children Playing in the Streets at weddings and funerals (Matthew 11,16f paralleled in Luke 7,31f) corresponds in detail with what actually occurred in Palestine 2,000 years ago, as the children played their games. One also sensed the relevance of the timeless underlying message when applied contextually, which in the case of this example might be summed up as: "There are always those who avoid responsibility by remaining on the sidelines and criticising anyone who poses a challenge to their escapism." (For a fuller discussion on the interpretation of this parable see Jeremias, 1954, p. 160f, also Hunter, 1960, p. 77, and Dodd, 1961, p. 24f.)

The critical tools used to handle the Bible with integrity should not be undervalued, neither should their lessons be forgotten; they still have value when carefully used but scholarly approaches to understanding the writings of Scripture have moved on, especially in allowing a creative interaction between the reader and the text and in encouraging a more imaginative interpretation.

It is the "moving on" factor that is of particular importance for the theme in hand. I shall not at this point attempt a comprehensive review of this significant development; to do so would take a lot of space without having a direct bearing on the course of this book. I shall, rather, cut to the quick and pick an aspect of this development which does have a direct bearing.

During the last, approximately, thirty years, allowing for the inevitable overlap that occurs in scholarly developments, a number of interrelated approaches to the reading of the Bible have developed and it is this cluster of disciplines, each a tributary in itself, that is commonly referred to as *literary criticism*. This approach, as already noted, is not confined to and did not originate with the reading of sacred texts. Its primary function, as the title suggests, is to look at the subject matter *as literature*. However, it soon became established as a significant way of responding to the question about how we read the Bible. The following comment indicates the tenor of *literary criticism* and its relationship to earlier disciplines: "What distinguishes modern criticism from earlier descriptive research…is its inquiry into how texts communicate, and what constitutes meaning…" (Davies, 1990a, p. 402).

From our perspective, the critical factor in the application of modern literary criticism to the Bible, is the focus it places on the reader. Speaking at first of the general application of literary criticism and then with specific reference to the Bible, Davies says:

> …literary criticism has shifted its focus of attention from the author, to the text itself, and thence to the reader. A parallel movement can be traced in the literary criticism of the Bible. The change began because the current explanation of how writings convey meanings to readers was seen to be inadequate. This explanation claimed that the author's intention gives meaning to a text, and that the reader must discover the author's intention to gain understanding. [p. 402]

Davies' most telling comment, as far as the focus of this book is concerned, is a statement about intentionality and again, although

the context of this comment is secular literature, it applies equally
to the Bible:

> ...literary critics began to express doubts about defining the meaning of a
> text through the discovery of the author's intention. Although the author
> may be assumed to have an intention, or a number of different intentions,
> in writing a book, he or she may neither be fully aware of those intentions
> nor fulfil them in the work. [p. 403]

The last quotation in particular and especially the reference to an
author's *unawareness*, offers a creative and exciting pathway to
an interaction between literary criticism and a psychodynamic
approach. The idea that an author may not be *fully aware* of her or
his intention flows right into the depths of unconscious processes, a
vital aspect of any psychodynamic psychology.

We need now to look briefly at one other strand of literary criticism
which resonates with our theme and amplifies the point made about
unconscious processes. In fact it almost brings us to a place where we
can begin to see and enjoy the complementarity of psychology and
religion and apply its approach to specific areas of interest.

Reader-Response Criticism is one of the developments in biblical
interpretation which has opened the door to a more imaginative
handling of the Bible. Specifically, it has offered a natural bridge
to a psychodynamic approach to reading Scripture. Once again the
term applies not to a clearly defined tradition but to an emphasis
found within several approaches to reading literature, of which
sacred texts are one. The sources for this approach can be traced as
far back as the 1940s and even before that we get a clear indication
of the flavour of *reader-response criticism*. The following quote has a
fresh, contemporary feel about it and yet was written in 1938 on the
subject of reading literature. The author is insisting that the teacher
of literature must take care not to impose: "...preconceived notions
about the proper way to react to any work." [Rather], "the student
must be free to grapple with his own reaction... to be given the
opportunity and the courage to approach literature personally, to let
it mean something to him directly" (Rosenblatt, 1938, p. 66).

Reader-response criticism, therefore, developed during the last fifty
years as a reaction to, as well as alongside, other more objective or
historically-focused approaches. It is illuminating and relevent to
read that this imaginative approach to literature has an intrinsic

relation to psychology: "Reader-Response Criticism ...is based on gestalt psychology" (Davies, 1990b, p. 579). Gestalt psychology is a distinctive "school" of therapy but the point to note here is that it is thoroughly psychodynamic in its approach. Davies' article on Reader-Response Criticism is a helpful introduction to the subject, especially as it is illustrated by reference to a biblical passage (578f).

For the purposes of this book, the Reader-Responsive approach gives credence to what we might simply term, a more imaginative interaction with biblical texts and stories and more widely, Christian doctrine. In particular, might this allow for the influence of unconscious processes within those texts and stories, so that without detaching ourselves from what is recorded, or bypassing its historical context, what is not written – the "gaps" or "blanks", as Wolfgang Iser terms it – provide a creative place in which the reader interprets what is being read? Iser argues that texts contain gaps (or blanks) that powerfully affect the reader, who must explain them, connect what they separate, and create in his or her mind aspects of a work that are not in the text but are incited by the text. (Iser, 1978). Is this all that far removed from what is meant when we speak of reading between the lines?

Might the above also mean that we no longer need to be absolutely sure that this or that interpretation was intended, or that the writer was consciously aware of the full import of all that his or her words conveyed? I would argue that any imaginative interpretation should have an intrinsic relatedness to the text; it must in some way link with what might have been going on in the story, even if it was not recognised at the time, or by the writer or editor of that story. In a book referred to earlier, the writer meditates on the biblical story of "the last supper" and in particular the act of treachery by Judas Iscariot who, in the middle of the meal and of the night, leaves to betray Jesus, (see The Gospel of John 13,30). As a therapist, Thorne poses the imaginative thought as to why no one questions Judas, if – as it appears in the story – some are aware of his intentions? By bringing this psychological perspective to bear on the story, the reader is reminded of the all-too-human failing of "corporate betrayal". (Thorne, 1991, p. 11f). "Scape-goating", "passing the buck", projection (of our own failings onto another) and allowing others to do our "dirty work", all resonate in this context.

The above point about unconscious processes is of special importance for the credence of this book's theme because it gives a flavour of the complementarity between the worlds of psychology and religion that I shall give more developed examples of later. The importance of unconscious communication is fundamental to most counselling therapies and their theoretical underpinning. One of the most masterly works in this area, which is relevant to the particular complementarity of this book's theme, is Bruno Bettleheim's *The Uses of Enchantment* (Bettleheim, 1976), in which the author demonstrates in fine detail and by analysing several well known fairy tales, how the real power of these stories is their ability to communicate psychological truth to a child regarding relationships, at *an unconscious level*. The importance of the unconscious in this process is that it is unwritten and therefore implicit. It is not therefore forced onto the child's mind but allowed to register, as the child requires and unconsciously "chooses". The young child, for example, who has natural, healthy, ambiguous feelings of love and hatred towards her/his mother is able to safely find an outlet for the hatred by unconsciously identifying mother with the archetypal Witch, Wicked Queen/Step-mother etc of fairy tales. The fairy tale, says Bettleheim: "...is therapeutic because the patient finds his *own* solutions, through contemplating what the story seems to imply about him and his inner conflicts at this moment in his life (Bettleheim, 1976, p. 25).

In the fairy tale of The Three Little Pigs, for example:

The wolf...is obviously a bad animal, because it wants to destroy. The wolf's badness is something the young child recognizes within himself: his wish to devour, and its consequence – the anxiety about possibly suffering such a fate himself. So the wolf is an externalization, a projection of the child's badness – and the story tells how this can be dealt with constructively. [*ibid*, p. 44]

Bettleheim draws strong comparisons between his study and what he sees as the aims of religion::

If there is a central theme to the wide variety of fairy tales, it is that of a rebirth to a higher plane (179) and earlier: ...many Biblical stories are of the same nature as fairy tales. The conscious and unconscious associations which fairy tales evoke in the mind of the listener depend on his general frame of reference and his personal preoccupations. Hence, religious persons will find in them much of importance that is not mentioned here. [*ibid*, p. 13]

Perhaps then, what is rather loosely termed *reader-responsive criticism* might help to free the person of faith to read the faith stories of the Bible more imaginatively and allow for unconscious processes when doing so.

We are now ready to look at the particular perspectives of theology and therapy which I shall use as my areas in which convergence and complementarity occur.

PART II

Theological and Therapeutic Perspectives

CHAPTER FOUR

A theological perspective: panentheism

In this chapter I want to make a brief journey along a particular theological stream. In the following chapter I shall take a similar course with psychology. The first stream is my own theology, or less ambitiously, my theological perspective. I cannot assume that others will feel at home in this stream, though some may. Nevertheless, the streams others travel may have some similarities to mine, since all streams share similar properties. Perhaps our streams intersect at several points and for a while flow into each other. Perhaps they converge to form a broader, well established river, which in turn converges with other rivers, and eventually flows into the sea, and into the vast ocean of religion. In proposing this perspective, I cannot disown or ignore the accompanying myriad of tributaries, streams and rivers with which I mix along the way. I need to connect with other, larger experiences than mine; to know and feel part of the greater whole. In the context of this book this will not seduce me into attempting a definition of religion but I will have to demonstrate how my theological perspective can be supported as a genuine expression of what religion, at heart, is about.

The above comments expose me to the criticism of being too subjective. This dilemma is not as crushing as it may first appear. Any debate between psychology and religion depends on the contributor's experience, perceptions and convictions and the reader is invited to assess whether the definitions of either or both have integrity. I am not speaking here of finely-tuned, literalistic definitions of either religion or counselling/therapy. Neither am I wanting to argue that other definitions are not valid; enshrined in my own theology and my understanding of healing processes, is the belief that no one person, or one belief system, can at best do more than shed light on what we rather glibly call "the truth". This view is not negative or reductionist but actually says something essential and therefore positive about the nature of authentic religious experience. That "something" is expressed with powerful brevity in a statement which has a contemporary feel but which was coined in the 18th century: "A God comprehended is no God" (Tersteegen, 1917, p. 39).

The view above does not excuse me, or others, from making informed judgements about the authenticity of differing facets of both religious faith and therapeutic counselling and this will inevitably involve challenging what we consider to be discrepancies, particularly between what is being claimed and what we observe and experience. When the waters are murky or stagnant, we cannot shirk the responsibility of saying so. Regarding religion, Jung writes at some length on this subject., recognising the distortions of religion and yet how the distortions themselves may have an important role within society:

> What is usually and generally called "religion," is to such an amazing degree a substitute that I ask myself seriously whether this kind of "religion", which I prefer to call a creed, has not an important function in human society. [Jung, 1938, p. 52]

Jung, by defining what he sees as "a substitute" let's us know something about his view of authentic religion:

> The substitution has the obvious purpose of replacing immediate experience by a choice of suitable symbols invested in a solidly organized dogma and ritual. The Catholic church maintains them by her indisputable authority, the Protestant church...by insistence upon faith and the evangelical message. As long as those two principles work, people are effectively defended and shielded against immediate religious experience. [*ibid.*, p. 52f]

It is clear from this that Jung sees one of the chief marks of any religion as "immediate" (spiritual) experience. The sociologist and in some respects the psychologist, will try to "tell it as it is"; neither is primarily concerned about credibility gaps between what is observed and what is desirable, or what is preached and what is practised. Freud, for example, in his dialogue with religion, is not concerned to tell us what religion should be but rather, what he observes it to be and the functions it serves in that way. I am making no apologies for being more akin to the approach of Jung and to the (more recent) views of Pruyser, in which describing religion clearly involves an attempt to define what is considered to be "good" and "bad" religion, the quotation from Jung being an example.

In the closing brief chapter of Pruyser's *Dynamic Psychology of Religion*, entitled *Some Perennial Problems*, the first section is *Difficulties in Defining Religion* (Pruyser, 1968, p. 329f). I do not find myself in complete agreement with Pruyser, after consideration of his points. Pruyser is reluctant to include, in his definition of religion, too much of that which is "private", by which he means, the religious experience of the individual. He appears to be seeking to redress the imbalance, as he sees it, in other writers, not least it appears, William James, whose classic *Varieties* Pruyser nevertheless describes as "brilliant". Pruyser writes:

> My fourth guide has been the recognition that religion is both private and public, individual and institutional, subjective and objective. Religion is not merely an intimate and deeply personal feeling, or a highly idiosyncratic belief. It has a visible apparatus in buildings, books, schools, organizations, holidays, instruments, art products, and programs in the mass media. It has departments in universities, academic degrees, and a vast body of scholarly studies. It has orthodox and liberal wings. It has enormous libraries. All these features must be taken into account in a useful definition of religion. However, the distinctions between the private and public aspects of religion do not coincide with the division between the psychological and sociological disciplines. Therefore, the psychology of religion cannot confine itself to the private side of religious experience... Hence I have deliberately avoided placing too much stress on religious *experience*, since that term suggests a preoccupation with the private at the expense of the corporate aspects of religion. [*ibid.*, p. 333]

I entirely agree with the emphasis which Pruyser makes in this passage but in doing so he seems to give the impression that "private" and "personal" are synonymous terms. I have indicated earlier (see Introduction par. 4) that there is a subtle but important difference.

Aside from the above misgivings, I believe that Pruyser strikes the right balance in arguing for a broad definition of "religion". At the risk of being guilty of a contradiction in terms, we might say that it is, an undefined definition. Using the world of art as a comparison, Pruyser writes:

> Theories of aesthetics and definitions of the beautiful abound, but they are of little avail to students who want to set up clear boundaries to "art" as a field of investigation. Indeed, the use of spatial terms such as "field" and "boundaries" is inadequate, for neither art nor religion is a territorial affair. The photographic term "focus" is better in that it leaves room for sharp centering as well as blurred edges and thus keeps a necessary amount of unclarity "in the picture. [*ibid.*, p. 329]

Pruyser's closing words on the subject, show that despite his caution regarding an excess of "personal feeling", he acknowledges his own experience as being a significant factor in his *perspectival definition* of "religion" and in light of my own personal convictions, expressed earlier, it will be apparent that I am in full agreement with Pruyser:

> ...despair at finding a concise verbal definition of religion does not mean surrender to chaos. One can work within a tradition which has its own implied or explicit formulations about religion, or its own selective focus. There are schools of thought in which global ideas gradually become articulated. While I do not claim membership in any school, *I know that I have in the course of years aligned myself with certain viewpoints and convictions, and have become loyal to a few leading ideas.* [*ibid.*, p. 334, my italics]

The reality is that any attempt to define religion (let alone psychotherapeutic convictions) in some absolute sense, is fraught with difficulties and doomed to failure, for we are not talking here of sociological, historical, or even ecclesiastical descriptions but rather asking questions about what makes religious faith authentic. Such a venture cannot result in precise, clearly defined conclusions. It is more akin to the childhood game of "getting warmer". Jung's description of "substitute" religion is for him the cry of "cold, cold, colder". In other words, the seeker of faith is involved in an existential journey. The journey requires the utmost commitment to understanding, learning and debate and is always respectful and valuing of the traditions that have been faithfully passed down to us through the centuries. Nevertheless, even with all this, we are left poised on the edge of a precipice. Kierkegaard reminds us that authentic religious faith, "requires a "leap" of faith, and this cannot be made for any man, it must be made by him" (Gates, 1961, p. 99).

Bearing all this in mind I will attempt to venture. In doing so I will not pretend to offer a "definition" of religion but rather, will indicate a theological context in which I will sketch my personal perspective and in doing so, I acknowledge that over the years I too have, inevitably, adhered to certain ideas, perhaps at times in a dogged and blinkered way.

I could, in an attempt to keep things simple but avoid simplicity, begin from one or other of two areas: the beliefs, theology and doctrines of a particular religion, or alternatively, its practices, life-style and ethics. If I may assume that integrity – both in the sense of that which is holistic, as well as that which is real and true to itself – is going to be foremost in any religious quest, I would have to conclude that these two areas (of belief and practice) must feed and inform each other; they must enjoy a fit, or at least strive for one, which has little or no trace of discrepancy. It is more than just interesting that what allows us to trust the other, whether the other be an individual, a group, an organization, a political party, or a religion, is whether or not what is believed, promised, or preached, is lived out, fulfilled and practised. It is also interesting that if we take the central figure of Christian religion, the "sin" he seems to consider most deadly is hypocrisy. Hypocrisy hardly needs explaining. We dislike it in ourselves and in others and of all failings it is the one which we would least wish to be accused of. Hypocrisy is more than being dishonest and goes deeper than moral failure. Hypocrisy is about not being true to ourselves and most of us value and yearn to be true to ourselves.

There are sayings which when first heard have an almost shocking but enlightening effect and which the hearer carries over the years and never forgets. Luther's: "Be a sinner and sin boldly..." is for me, such a saying. I have deliberately quoted only the first half of the saying, since that is how it is often presented, or rather misrepresented. Of course the complete quote is needed for a grasp of its meaning: *Esto peccator et pecca fortiter, sed fortius fide et guade in Christo*: Be a sinner and strong in your sins, but be stronger in your faith and rejoice in Christ (in a Letter to Melanchthon, *The Penguin Dictionary of Quotations*, 1960, p. 239). The translation with which am more familiar is: "Be a sinner and sin boldly, but believe and rejoice in Christ even more boldly, for he is victorious over sin, death, and the world." It is not entirely incidental to suggest that here is a saying which benefits from a *reader-responsive criticism* approach; whatever Luther intended I have always intuitively found in his injunction, a call to be realistic, in both an assessment of oneself and of the promises of one's faith. We do ourselves or others no good by pretending that we are something or someone other than we are.

The comments above are a reminder that it hardly matters whether we make our starting point theoretical or practical, theological or ethical; a mark of authentic religion and the religious person, is integrity. If the theory cannot be translated into practice it is a faulty theory. Theology, to be worthy of the name, has to be not only studied but lived. I shall continue this exploration by making some further theological comments, before looking at a framework, or perspective, for an understanding of a psychodynamic psychology but for both these subjects the practical application of theories must be evident throughout, both implicitly and explicitly.

If the model of religious faith I am working with was thoroughly theistic, in a conventional sense, with a categorical affirmation of God as an objective being (albeit, the most perfect and powerful of beings) then a psychodynamic understanding of human nature would not suggest the complementarity I have in mind and which I find so meaningful. It is in part because my theology is not based on a conventional theistic view that such an approach has become apparent to me. I hope that without further qualification the truth of that statement will become clear as we continue.

I make no attempt to hide my own theological stance. Indeed, It is essential to disclose this stance in order for any sort of comparison to be meaningful. Some may feel that I am open to the criticism of making my theology fit my psychology and vice versa. I can do no more than offer both my theological and psychological convictions, as they presently stand and claim that I am not attempting to make something fit but expressing what I find to be a genuine complementarity. As well as this being of significant personal value, it is, at least in principle, also of importance for both Christian apologetics and the view that there is a coherence within human experience. Einstein's theory of relativity might therefore be seen in much wider terms than the realm of physics; or to put it within the context of this discourse, the Christological claim of Colossians that *"in him all things hold together"* (Colossians 1,17), or its equivalent catchphrase attributed to Tertullian (an African

"Church Father", c.160—220 AD), *"Christ is the glue of society"*, may have a complementarity with what therapists refer to variously as, *maturation, individuation* or *integration*. Of course, part of being real is to accept that we can never be entirely free of bias, prejudice and error. The reader will need to assess what rings true for them by sifting the gold from the dross, or by creating what is for them a more authentic picture of religion and of psychology.

In attempting to indicate a view that provides a meaningful theological description of faith, I have named integration and authenticity (as opposed to hypocrisy) as hallmarks. I have also said that I do not breathe the theological air of pure theism but have so far not indicated an alternative. I shall now fill out the picture, conscious that it is personal to me but encouraged by the knowledge that it is shared by others and hoping that it may be of help to those who are seeking to change, expand, or reframe their own view.

My own quest for theological meaning has always necessitated trying to ask the right questions. One such question, framed in this context, is: "What is real, not merely as *a useful neurotic and even psychotic symptom* (Braungardt, 1999) but real in the sense of being believable; something I can allow to shape my life and life-style, something I am prepared to die for, or perhaps more importantly, to live for?" What I personally value and therefore retain, in Theism, is the accent on God being personal and responsive but in other respects the term is not sufficiently dynamic.

If not theism – strictly speaking – what are the remaining options, at least, in philosophical terms? I do not subscribe to pantheism, in which God and nature are equivalent, for this does no justice to an experience of God as transcendent, holy and unable to be contained. What then remains, in philosophical terms, which avoids the static aspects of conventional theism and the reductionism of pantheism? I have for many years now found myself comfortable with the philosophical concept of pan*en*theism (my italics). This concept is formally described as:

> The belief that the Being of God includes and penetrates the whole universe, so that every part of it exists in Him, but (as against Pantheism) that His Being is more than, and is not exhausted by, the universe. [Cross, 1957, p. 1010],

or as the advert for a quality car put it, *greater than the sum of its parts*. F.C.K Krause (1781—1832) was, according to Cross, the first to use the term *panentheism* (1010). In my use of the term I am not seeking to rigorously adhere to any philosophical system but to suggest a philosophical indicator which allows for the paradox that God is, *at one and the same time*, transcendent and immanent. The language of the Bible literally describes God as separated and self-contained; a God who sends his messengers, or who descends (from Heaven) himself, in one form or another but who similarly withdraws or ascends to his dwelling place. I take this to be a mythical way of pointing to the *difference* of God (Being Itself) from creation and creatures (beings) rather than a God who is *distant*.

The theology I am advocating is rooted in the biblical stories and has always been present within Christian thinking. This is the reason why I wish to distinguish carefully between "traditional" and "conventional". An example of an attempt to move beyond a conventional theology to a more dynamic, expansive one, emerges, in the 1960s, in John Robinson's concept of God as the *ground of our being*. (Robinson, 1963). Robinson was, in this respect, drawing on the theology of Paul Tillich, a German philosophical theologian, (1886—1965). In the realm of systematic theology, Tillich's terminology is improved upon (or rather, comprehensibly rejected!) by John Macquarrie's *existential, ontological theism*: "…we entirely avoid Tillich's notion of the "ground of being" which suffers not only from resembling too much the static idea of substance but is in addition, as I have shown elsewhere, thoroughly ambiguous." (Macquarrie, 1966, p. 100).

Macquarrie's ground-breaking work in systematic theology, first published more than forty years ago, makes a radical departure from previous presentations, not only because of the way in which it holds together in paradoxical tension models of "natural" and "revelation" theology but for inviting us to think about the language we use to describe God. Drawing upon Kant, Aristotle and Hegel to support his proposals, Macquarrie meticulously distinguishes between beings and "Being itself" and in turn, distinguishes the latter phrase from the concept of "substance". "Being" (in contrast to beings) is that which "lets be": "The expression which I prefer to use,…to point to the characteristic of being as the condition that there may be any particular beings, is "letting-be" (*ibid.*, p. 103).

Macquarrie's mammoth work gave those of us who trained theologically in the 1960s a new lease of theological life. It was more – much more – than a different, more accurate way of using god-language; it was an exciting and inspiring way of having and living faith. It had the particular strength of emphasising both the *difference* (transcendence) of God (from beings) and God's identity and involvement with beings (*immanence*). It was alive, dynamic and relational.

Should we regard Macquarrie's "new" formulation as an outright rejection of theism or a radical restatement? My own preference is for the latter and it is clear that that is Macquarrie's view:

> But does the equation of God with being and denial that he is a being not amount to atheism? To this it may be replied that the word "atheism" must always be understood in relation to what it denies. Presumably most modern men deny the gods of mythology, and so from the point of view of a believer in these gods, they are atheists. Likewise, one may suppose, the denial that God is a being would seem to be atheism to one who believes that there is such a being. I have spoken of an "existential-ontological theism" as distinct from "traditional (or metaphysical) theism." This existential-ontological theism is opposed to its own corresponding atheism. This atheism is the denial of the holiness of being, and consequently the denial that man should have faith in being or take up the attitude of acceptance and commitment before being. The distinction between the believer and the atheist, or between faith and unfaith, is just as clear in existential-ontological theism as it was in metaphysical theism, and is perhaps more important, for here atheism, like faith itself, gets understood not so much in terms of accepting or denying a world view as in terms of taking up an existential attitude. [*ibid.*, p. 107f]

In the realm of systematic theology, Macquarrie's influence is not difficult to find. One of the best articulations of this view is to be found in the writings of David F. Ford, professor of divinity at Cambridge: "God is not an object in the world to be related to other objects, but is often best understood as the condition for the possibility of the existence of anything and the understanding and practice of anything" (Ford, 2003, p. 10).

Macquarrie's thinking and those who developed their theology in a similar way, might find a good deal of resonance with what is referred to loosely as "Celtic Christianity"; a somewhat nebulous phrase but reflected at its best, I think, in the liturgy, theology, ministry and life-style of the Iona Community, with its emphasis on the presence of God within the natural world.

However disparate the above theologies may appear, they have in common an emphasis on the biblical concept of incarnation. The mythical nature of this concept is the language of a God who comes and goes; the truth within the myth is that God, by nature, is eternally incarnated – Being itself – woven into the inner fabric of all beings. George McLeod, founder of the Iona community, once described the historic island as "a thin place". It is perhaps fitting, especially if one believes in the importance of paradox and mystery, that no one is quite sure what McLeod meant! It is certain however that he wasn't referring simply to the geography of the island. He is saying something about the thin "line", between the material and the spiritual, the transient and the intransient, the earthly and the heavenly, which some pilgrims to the island experience: "Iona has been described a "a thin place", only a tissue paper separating the material from the spiritual." (Ferguson, 1988, p. 16). George Herbert (1593—1633) reminds us that the thought has a long history:

> A man that looks on glass
> On it may stay his eye;
> Or if he pleaseth, through it pass,
> And then the heaven espy.

(*Hymns and Psalms*, 1983, n. 803, *Teach me, my God and King*, 2nd verse).

I have tried to indicate a theological perspective which makes sense to me, both in terms of the biblical record, the testimony of others – past and present – and of my own faith experience. With this in mind the reader will, I hope, understand what I mean, without necessarily agreeing with me at every point, when referring to Christian concepts, as I seek to compare them with psychodynamic thinking.

CHAPTER FIVE

A psychological perspective:
psychodynamic therapy

As far as I know, unlike the subject of our last chapter, no blood has been shed over the differences within psychotherapy and counselling during its relatively brief history, although rivalry and wrangling has long since left its mark. For a good overview of the turbulent history of psychoanalysis in Great Britain see Peter Fuller's "Introduction" to *Psychoanalysis and Beyond* (Rycroft, 1985, pp. 1—38). The contemporary scene of counselling services and of counselling training courses accessible to the general public, can be confusing to say the least. I shall resist the temptation of attempting to offer an overview of this complex array of counselling therapies since to do so would lead us away from the main aim in this chapter which is to indicate a psychodynamic perspective for using alongside the theological one of Chapter 4. It is as though a pair of spectacles were being made; a religious lens has been created and now a psychological one is needed. I have already prescribed a distinctive tint for this lens – the theory and practice of psychodynamic therapy – but that tells the reader little about how the lens is actually constructed. I shall now turn to this task, accepting that it will be just as much a personal prescription as the theological lens.

Many forms of counselling, which go under different names, nevertheless share a psychodynamic approach. The reason for this is that the term "psychodynamic" is a broad one, which encompasses many aspects of psychology and psychological development. Therapies, for example, which use music, drama or art, may have a specific title but all may be based on, or incorporate, a strong psychodynamic element. Other counselling models embrace a psychodynamic approach but have an orientation to a particular tradition or a famous pioneering figure in the history of psychotherapy – Freudian, Kleinian, Alderian, Jungian; Gestalt therapy, Person-Centred (or Client-Centred) counselling, Transactional Analysis and Integrative counselling. All these and many more, distinct as they may be, are either thoroughly or partially psychodynamic.

In light of the above, the reader may have lost sight of the wood for the trees. What might help at this point is to give an indication – I can promise no more since the term is intended to be a broad one – of what is meant by *psychodynamic* counselling, in particular. Psychodynamic counselling derives from the tradition of psychoanalysis which developed in the United Kingdom during the last century and has its origins in the pioneering work of the two (distinctly different) figures of Sigmund Freud and Carl Jung. It does not, however, align itself entirely with either of these and is not therefore "Freudian" or "Jungian", in the sense that some therapists are. The psychodynamic tradition developed under the influence of a "school" commonly called "Object Relations", the origins of which are to be found in the work of Melanie Klein, whose theories will be looked at shortly. Some of the later and more commonly recognized figures of the Object Relations school are Donald Winnicott, Ronald Fairbairn, Harry Guntrip, Michael Balint and John Bowlby. The latter of these figures is also famous for the development of *Attachment Theory* and is particularly distinct from the others.

The Object Relations school, which helped shape the psychodynamic approach, differs from traditional psychoanalytical theory and particularly from Freud, in one major respect. Freud's understanding of how we function as human beings is based on his belief that we always seek to avoid pain and distress and find satisfaction. This process is driven by the *id* (Freud's word for the amoral, libidinal-aggressive forces within us) and is active unconsciously. Freud called the process, the *Pleasure Principle,* which is in conflict with, or regulated by, the *Reality Principle.* The latter is driven by the *ego* – the conscious self – which has the ability to harness and rein in the *Id* so that the ego has some control over the id and prevents it from running wild, so to speak. This theory effectively means that though we may wish to think of our motives and behaviour as altruistic, other people and relationships (often referred to in developmental psychology as *objects*, as in *Object Relations*) are the means through which we achieve pleasure. *Object Relations* theory, especially in its developments beyond Klein (who always saw herself as a true interpreter of Freud) effectively turns the above principle around so that the driving force within human behaviour is to achieve relationship and secure attachments; these become the goal of our strivings, even though we may seek them in the most pleasurable way possible. I have always thought that if, as is said, "truth be known", Freud's pleasure principle and the theories of object relations are not diametrically opposed but paradoxically joined, or to put it another way: as human beings, we need to accept that we have mixed motives and are driven by conflicting forces. If this is so, the critical issue would be an awareness of these conflicts that would in turn enable us to act more out of choice and thereby realistically and responsibly.

Despite the multiplicity of psychological theories and some fundamental differences of opinion, there is a consensus, broadly speaking, within psychodynamic thinking of what characterizes this approach. The following is by no means an exhaustive list and the reader familiar with the subject may wish to add more: the reality of *unconscious experience*, the psychological processes of *introjection, projection, projective identification, transference* and *countertransference*, the importance of *boundaries*, external and internal and the *dynamic and inter-related nature of the human psyche*, including especially the profound influences of our past experience, often in the shape of unresolved, painful feeling, on our present behaviour and in our relationships.

These insights can be applied, whether they are seen in terms of a Freudian stages model of human development, insights of the Object Relations school, or a particular development of that school, such as John Bowlby's attachment-based theory, with its emphasis on ethology and the life-long importance of attachment-seeking and separation anxiety. The following extended quote may help those not familiar with ethology or its particular use in the work of Bowlby and *attachment theory*:

> Reading *King Solomon's Ring* (Lorenz, 1952) introduced [Bowlby] to the new science of ethology, the biological study of animal behaviour from evolutionary and functional perspectives. This was the period of imprinting and critical periods. Separation experiments with monkeys showed that

those deprived of a parent-figure were unable to mate or parent young; and offered the choice between a wire-frame "mother" which dispensed milk and one which was more comforting, young monkeys overwhelmingly preferred the cloth-covered frame...These studies proved that contrary to Kleinian and Freudian assumptions, attachment was not a derivative of feeding and was essential for emotional maturation. [Gomez, 1997, p. 154]

I stated earlier in this chapter that I would consider the work of Melanie Klein, whose theories, as already noted, marked a turning point in the development of psychotherapy and particularly the development of a psychodynamic approach. This will serve to give an introduction to some of the concepts named above. I need to emphasise that by choosing Klein as a focus I am not implying that this is the only or best way; it is simply a helpful starting point, particularly since Klein's model of infant development resonates so strongly with our adult psychological problems and their damaging expressions in personal and social relationships, as well as in political policies and behaviour, globally. However, the work of Freud, Winnicott, Bowlby and others are never far from mind and are drawn upon frequently, implicitly as well as directly.

Melanie Klein occupies a distinct place in the history of psychoanalysis for a number of reasons, some of which have already been noted. One of the strengths of her work as an analyst is that she was the first major figure in the history of the development of psychoanalysis to base her clinical work with adults on direct observation of infants with their mothers. Building on Freud – though in the following respect Klein is: "more Freudian than the Freudians" (Rycroft, 1985, p. 15) Klein bases her understanding of the development of the ego and the personality, on what she calls (following Freud) the *life and death instincts*. The death instinct is the cause of persecutory anxiety and consequently, feelings of disintegration and the threat of annihilation. These feelings are initially focussed on the part object of the mother's bad breast, This experience is simultaneously introjected (or taken in), projected, re-introjected and again projected in a dynamic and continuous cycle: "...from the beginning object-relations are moulded by an interaction between introjection and projection..." (Klein, M. 1946a, p. 2). The life instinct, moving towards integration, operates in a similar way but is focussed on the good breast of the mother. The terminology, used by Klein, of good and bad breast can feel daunting and even a little bizarre to those who are not familiar with her writings. I do not want to fall into the trap of attempting to over-explain Klein. The most important point to remember at this stage is that these terms are used in a literal, physical sense and also, *simultaneously*, in a metaphorical, or symbolic way, as referring to how the child experiences the mother as the one on whom he/she depends utterly. The mother can therefore be experienced as one who feeds, nurtures and holds, or as one who withholds and acts towards her child in a vengeful and persecutory way. I need to stress that what is being described by Klein here is the reality of the infant's experience, not necessarily, or typically, the reality of the mother's intentions or behaviour towards her child.

The reasons for this strange, sharply contrasting experience of the baby is better understood when we remember that Klein is describing the infant's relationship to its mother in the earliest stage of a child's development when feelings are most intense and extreme. These experiences are largely separated since the ego cannot tolerate the ambivalence of good and bad existing in the same object. The need for the good breast – or we might say, a good experience of the mother – to be successfully introjected and integrated into the ego, necessitates psychic processes which Klein calls "splitting" and "idealisation": "Idealisation is bound up with the splitting of the object, for the good aspects of the breast are exaggerated as a safeguard against the fear of the persecuting breast" (Klein, M. 1946b, p. 7). Klein describes this earliest stage of development as the "paranoid-schizoid position". The second stage, which occurs approximately during the second half of the first six months of life, she calls "the depressive position", during which feelings become less intense and extreme and an experience of the mother, (or even the breast as a part object), as good and bad, begins to be accommodated.

Winnicott, acknowledging Klein's contribution, says of this stage: "A new capacity for object-relating has now been developed, namely, one that is based on an interchange between external reality and samples from the personal psychic reality" (Winnicott, 1971, p. 131). What Winnicott is alluding to here is a dynamic process which shapes our lives; how we respond within relationship, how cautious or otherwise we are and what degree of self-valuing we have. Therapists who work psychodynamically will know how this factor is at the heart of most, probably all, problems that clients present. Each of us carries the imprint – imagine if you can that we have an internal "map" – of what we have experienced. Of course the "map" is not entirely featureless when we are born but as we experience life, those experiences become written into our map, or they confirm, compound or contradict our experience, causing us to update our map. At its best this mapping, or internal, object-relating record, serves us well: "once bitten twice shy" is a catch-phrase reminding us that one of the ways in which we survive and thrive is because we have experiences which enable us to make sound judgements and to avoid danger in the future. In this case the "objects" referred to (internalized within ourselves) are "good objects". However, if the experiences we have, especially hurtful, confusing experiences, are not responded to at the time, they may become "bad", damaging, internal objects. If when bitten by the dog for the first time, there is no one to comfort and reassure us and to give us good, balanced guidance about dogs, "once bitten, twice shy", may easily become "twice bitten, terrified", and then, three times bitten equals "all dogs bite and are to be avoided at all costs, perhaps even exterminated." It requires the minimum of reflection to recognize the out-workings of that in adult life and relationships, in terms of prejudice, bigotry, persecution and ethnic cleansing.

The depressive position is so called because a realisation and accommodation of the ambivalence evokes feelings of guilt and a need for reparation within the child. Experience and acceptance of ambivalence, in oneself, in others and in relationships, also entails a fundamental loss; we are required to jettison the illusion that human beings are either unequivocally "good" or "bad". The acceptance, however, like all loss experiences, offers the opportunity of liberation from a static, defensive and unrealistic position to a more mature, realistic one.

It is important, in understanding Klein, and especially when applying her theories in clinical situations, to grasp her point that the splitting and idealisation, characteristic of the paranoid-schizoid position, is not absolute. Even at this stage a measure of ambivalence can be experienced, if only transitorily. In Klein's 1952 paper, there is a clear modification of her view in this direction: "I now consider that ambivalence, too, is already experienced in relation to part-objects" (Klein, 1952a, p. 66 f.n.1). Similarly, the two "positions" are not best viewed as categorical stages which are negotiated in strict chronological sequence; a better image might be overlapping areas or interlocking circles. So for Klein: "Some fluctuations between the paranoid-schizoid and depressive positions always occur and are part of normal development. No clear division between the two stages of development can therefore be drawn..." (Klein, 1946e, p. 16). Or in a later paper: "...persecutory and depressive anxieties, although conceptually distinct from one another, are clinically often mixed" (Klein, 1950, p. 45). It is also important to note that although these childhood experiences are to some extent (initially) worked through with varying degrees of success, they are "carried forward" by the individual and: "...to some extent indeed this applies to the whole of life" (Klein, 1952b, p. 80). This latter point is of enormous importance for it gives us many clues in understanding our attitudes and behaviour towards each other as adults. In particular and for the purposes of this study, it will help us to understand more clearly the unconscious processes within religious belief and practice, as well as beyond.

Inside out (projection)

The psychological process of projection is well attested by those who practise any form of psychoanalytical or psychodynamic therapy/ counselling. More so, it is one of those psychodynamic processes which has also become familiar in common parlance. In defending or commending a psychodynamic approach some concepts are relatively less easy to deal with than others; "projection" is, at least theoretically, one of the relatively easier ones. The intelligent enquirer (or protagonist) can often not only understand but accept the basic premise of projection as a common enough trait in our human behaviour. However, dealing with projection in practice is, invariably, much more difficult. Defensive (or coping) mechanisms often prevent us from consciously acknowledging our projections and even to do so does not necessarily lead to the withdrawing of those projections. Indeed, it is acknowledged that to do so entirely is practically impossible, given our need to manage pain, which we fear will overwhelm us if not kept at bay. This feared pain is often about feelings of humiliation, inadequacy, or even a fear of our goodness and power and the responsibility that entails. This latter point may at first seem odd but it is an important facet of projection that has a resonance in the complementarity of psychology and religion, and I will examine it more fully in Chapter 8.

Projection is one of the earliest and most fundamental concepts of any psychoanalytical understanding of human behaviour and is closely related to the more complex mechanisms of introjection, projective identification, transference and countertransference.

I find it useful in practice to hold in mind that any form of projection is a way of denying or avoiding painful inner feelings; it is one of the "ego defences" whereby we protect our psychic life. Central to any understanding of projection is how a person deals with the relationship between their "inside" and the "outside"; in projection the two become confused, or, in some cases, fused. One of the most helpful descriptions of this process I am aware of is offered by Robert de Board:

> Projection occurs when a person unconsciously attributes to another person a characteristic that is in fact his own. Personal feelings of dislike, hatred, or envy that one person feels towards another and which give rise to internal feelings of neurotic anxiety are projected on to that person. The result is that instead of feeling "I hate you", this is now experienced through projection as "you hate me". What was originally an internal threat is now experienced as an external threat and can be dealt with in the same way as all external threats, that is, by fight or flight...Projection blurs this boundary and distorts reality by making what is inside (within the self) appear to be outside. [de Board, 1978, p. 115f]

Although, as noted above, not all projections can be entirely withdrawn, maturation, or the individuation process, involves a greater understanding of what belongs to me and what belongs to others: "The effectiveness of the individual lies in knowing the boundary between the self and the outside world and perceiving what is inside and what is outside" (ibid., p. 116). Because, as stated above, projection is a coping mechanism, it is more readily observed in others than in oneself. One of the clues for detecting strong forms of projection, whether in others or ourselves, is to be aware of how vociferous and zealous a person's condemnation of another (or others) is. This "over the top" crusade-type condemnation is often a sign of how hard a person is working to fool themselves that a frightening and shameful feeling within, belongs outside; self-hatred is projected onto another or others who are then seen as dangerous, persecutory figures.

Jason, who was twenty seven and single, came to counselling in a tormented state. He described feelings of loathing he had towards gays and how it was disgusting that they should be allowed to flaunt their perversion in public places. His father, who had recently died, had often warned him to be on his guard against such men and to have nothing to do with them. "I idealized my father ", he said, "He knew what he was talking about." "It doesn't sound as though it was easy to disagree with your father?" I remarked. "I never needed to disagree" he said, in a rather angry tone. "I respected him. In any case we never answered back …. or else." "Or else what?" I enquired. "He'd take the strap to us… and we weren't allowed to cry…that was for girls, he would say… and: "I'll make a man of you." Something Jason had said earlier in this first meeting stuck in my mind and I ventured to put it to him. "You mentioned gay men in public places…You were thinking of…?" "Well…like bars…gay bars…" he said, with some awkwardness and embarrassment I thought. I risked saying: "You know of such places?" "Sure", replied Jason. "You don't have to be gay to go to them but everyone knows that's where they meet." It is difficult to convey the subtle but profound changes that took place for Jason within just three more sessions but as is frequently stated in psychodynamic training courses, "It is often all there in the first session." Over the following weeks Jason faced his dilemma. He had always felt more attracted to the same sex. This awareness became especially strong for him in his teenage years but he knew well his father's views; it was unthinkable that he might be gay. The truth is that Jason had known himself to be gay for many years but dare not allow himself to acknowledge it or perhaps even be aware of the reality. The session in which Jason broke down and sobbed was the turning point. He eventually voiced his repressed anger towards his father (for Jason, the flip side of the idealization), and acknowledged his true feelings. I met Jason unexpectedly, in a supermarket, a few years later. He proudly introduced me to Mark, his partner. They had been living together for the last two years.

Outside in (introjection)

Theoretically, it may be argued that introjection precedes projection; in reality the two are part of an inseparable cyclical experience. I have commented on the latter first only because of its familiarity.

The concept of introjection, though less of a household word, is of vital importance in a psychodynamic understanding of human behaviour. Indeed, both concepts are "two sides of the same coin". One cannot exist without the other, for if nothing is taken in (introjection) nothing can be pushed out (projection). For the purposes of this study, introjection will provide as valuable a clue to our theme of complementarity as projection.

On first encounter with the psychodynamic concept of introjection one can be mislead by its apparent simplicity. However, like its opposite side – projection – introjection is paradoxically simple and complex. The complexity is in large part due to the differing ways in which significant figures or "schools" of psychotherapy understand and use the term. Fortunately, there is sufficient similarity between these technical uses of introjection for me to choose the "simple" route and not become too led astray into complexity. With this in mind I shall attempt to convey the feel of introjection by putting it into my own words rather than regurgitating authoritative texts. In this way I hope that "introjection" will become less a theoretical mystery, accessible only to the initiated, and more of an experience which all of us know but have not perhaps been aware of.

I have already provided a backcloth for an understanding and experience of introjection earlier in this chapter, when talking about how we take things in and asking the reader to image having an internal map. We bring into this life inherited factors: physical likenesses to our parents, mannerisms etc. These are part of the given-ness of that internal map. What we have may indeed be a great deal but for sure there are spaces, or undeveloped parts. The modern computer motherboard looks crowded enough – if you've ever encountered it – but if you look closely you will find lots of room for development; sockets, expansion slots; drive and disk holders etc. For the newly conceived and newly born baby experiences rush in at an enormous rate. In the earliest stage of growth we appear to have little or no capacity for memory, in the cognitive way in which we normally speak of memory but we still take in our experiences; they impress themselves upon us; our internal map begins to acquire more and more detail. I call these impressions "feeling memories". They are enormously important for us but are not directly accessible to us through our normal, cognitive processes. However, listening to the life-stories of those who engage in counselling can provide reasonably clear indications of what life was like pre-cognitively. There may also be those alive, of our family, who can fill out the story. If a client/patient tells me that his earliest memory is of his elder sibling being beaten by their drunken alcoholic father, I have to assume that the alcoholism and its inevitable associated problems didn't began at that point but some while before.

After only a matter of months the internal map is alive with detail, built out of countless experiences, both good and bad. These experiences provide a "bank" of information which is automatically drawn upon to inform our responses when we encounter similar situations to ones in the past. In the case history I used in the section above on projection, Jason told me about his father using the strap to punish his children. This would have been a sure way for Jason to have quickly learned not to step out of line. Unfortunately, he learned his lesson through fear and the threat of violence which later prevented him from voicing how he felt.

What we take in, by way of experiences, has a profound effect on us. This then becomes the basis of how we also react to life in adulthood. It produces the strange experience, disclosed frequently in the counselling relationship of the client saying, "I know this sounds stupid but…" or "I feel so childish saying this…" This latter phrase is a particularly telling one and my answer is invariably "It feels like that because that is where the feeling began. You are responding as though you are still back there…and why not when you have not had much help to do otherwise?" I rarely come across anyone who doesn't understand this interpretation once they have been helped to do so. Like the woman client who stays in an abusive relationship, despite the "good advice" of caring friends. Abusive relationships are the norm for such people; they fear the unknown because they have come to believe that they are worth no more than the way in which they have been treated. So often the therapeutic "treatment" is a process of mourning the hitherto unspoken hurt, sadness and loss of the past, and beginning to move forward with greater self-esteem.

In this rough sketch of introjection I need to emphasise that the process works positively just as forcibly as negatively. The third and last of Freud's "parts" of his metaphorical description of the human psyche, which I chose not to include in my earlier comments in this chapter, is the *super ego*. Put simply, this is a way of pointing to those "shoulds" and "oughts", social and religious prescriptions and traditions, family "scripts" and instilled habits which sometimes haunt and pursue us and drive us to act unthinkingly, despite our yearning to be different. The point I want to make, however, is that the *super ego* will also carry positive, helpful material. Do you cringe and frown with disbelief when you witness someone openly dropping a sweet wrapper, drinks can, or cigarette packet, on the pavement? If you do it is probably because you were told from an early age to place any litter in a basket for that purpose. For myself the fond and grateful memory is my father's guidance about tram tickets. (If this doesn't make sense, ask someone older than yourself to explain!). "If you aren't able to put the ticket in the container on the tram as you get off, put it in your pocket and put it in the bin at home." Such things and far more important ones become "second nature".

I hope the above, somewhat disparate comments on introjection will nevertheless be of some help, especially when we come to consider the subject of the Holy Spirit in Chapter 9.

You in me and me in you (projective identification)

How does projective identification relate to and differ from projection? At this point I find relief in identifying with a frank statement of Patrick Casement's: "Unfortunately, it is not easy to get a clear understanding of projective identification from the literature alone, as this concept has become complicated by the varied uses to which it has been put." (Casement, 1985, p. 80). Despite this reticence – or perhaps because of it – I find Casement's subsequent remarks on projective identification, based on his clinical experience, some of the most helpful on the subject. Speaking of that aspect of projective identification which Casement calls "affective communication" (communication through feeling), he says:

> When projective identification is used *as a form of affective communication*, the projector has a need (usually unconscious) to make another person aware of what is being communicated and to be responded to. [*ibid.*, p. 81]

Sally was the client of a supervisee. She was in her middle thirties and had three children, the eldest, a girl of fourteen, and the two younger ones, had different fathers. Sally had divorced her first, abusive, husband. She continued a relationship with the younger children's father but he offered little support to them or her. Sally's childhood had not been good and she acknowledged in the counselling that she looked for love from her children as some kind of compensation for the love she had never received. Because of this she found it hard to give her children careful boundaries; to say "No" to them on occasions raised fears in her that she would lose their love. Consequently her parenting skills were poor and the domestic scene was regularly chaotic. In the session prior to supervision, Sally had told the counsellor, through her tears, that her eldest child was pregnant. The training counsellor was concerned that after several sessions working with Sally he felt totally stuck. "I feel powerless to help her, and what's worse, I find myself becoming bored and losing concentration. Every time she arrives for a session she looks totally depressed – beaten down – and says "Nothing's changed." I feel inadequate."

There was certainly no easy resolution to this client's problems but in the supervision we were able to identify the probable cause of the counsellor's feelings of impotence and near despair: They reflected powerfully how Sally was feeling. She was (quite unconsciously) dumping her feelings on the counsellor; making him feel how she felt. In doing this Sally was "unloading", making someone else feel the weight of her burden and in doing so was, as Casement points out in the above quote, wanting to have her sense of despair "responded too". The counsellor had become drawn into trying to "save" her, or solve her problems. After the next session he felt less weighed down and more involved with Sally and in his words, "More empathic". He stopped trying to be a problem solver and focussed on listening to Sally's despair, staying with it and letting her know how awful it sounded to feel so unsupported.

Projective identification, it should be noted, involves not only the so called bad parts of the self; that which is split off and projected can be "good":

> A part of the self that cannot be accepted by the subject is located in an object, another person. A projection is made to fit and to stick by relating to that person as if he were in reality a true representative of that split-off part of the self, as if he or she were truly disgusting, feeble, aggressive, ideal, or what have you. [Pines, 1983, p. 164].

Though having emphasised the word "ideal" in this quote, as an example of "good", I remind myself that the counterpart of idealization is often repressed anger.

Klein herself stresses, unequivocally, the positive aspect of projective identification:

> It is, however, not only the bad parts of the self which are expelled and projected, but also good parts of the self. Excrements then have the significance of gifts; and parts of the ego which, together with excrements, are expelled and projected into the other person represent the good, i.e. the loving parts of the self. The identification based on this type of projection again vitally influences object-relations. The projection of good feelings and good parts of the self into the mother is essential for the infant's ability to develop good object-relations and to integrate his ego. [Klein, 1946c, p. 8f]

There is however, as adults, a negative way in which we use projective identification to avoid the good in ourselves, a point made above in the discussion on projection. Counsellors and therapists are familiar with clients who cannot easily tolerate any sense of their own worth. To do so would fly in the face of how that person has been treated in the past and court the perceived probability of being treated like it again. In other words it is considered safer to sabotage one's hopes and aspirations, rather than risk the possibility of having these dashed. In such cases the fear of embracing and taking responsibility for one's own goodness is projectively identified into another, in the form of idealization. As I have commented above, the counterpart of idealization is often repressed anger, for there remains the yearning to enjoy and take responsibility for one's own goodness. These thoughts on projective identification will be vital in the discussion about salvation, in Chapter 8.

Back to the future (transference and countertransference)

The above process (of projective identification) involves being aware of transference, an unconscious process present in all human relationships but particularly thrown into relief and explored within the psychoanalytical setting. In transference, feelings about a past relationship are attributed to someone in the present. This will involve a projection by the client. It will sometimes take the form of projective identification, when the client not only projects feelings onto the counsellor but also identifies with those feelings, in her or him – a dumping process. The client also evokes feelings in the counsellor – the process of countertransference. These feelings may be the result of the client's projective identification (as in the relationship of the training counsellor and Sally), or may arise from the counsellor's "blind spots", prejudices and personal history. Transference and countertransference highlight what is being resonated within the relationship.

Projection, introjection, projective identification, transference and countertransference, are not separate psychic functions, one following the other, but are invariably intertwined in a complex and subtle dynamic. There is a sense in which one function is taken up and used within another, like the size-graded plastic beakers which we play with as small children. We might see transference and countertransference as a large outer beaker, slotted immediately on top of one called Projective Identification. Beneath this and within both, lies introjection and projection. This follows Casement's approximation: "I find it helpful to think of projective identification as a more powerful form of projection" (Casement, 1985, p. 81). Similarly, from Gomez: "Projective Identification is a more complex and extreme form of projection…" (Gomez, 1997, p. 38).

To describe transference as responding to the counsellor as if she/ he were a significant person in the client's past is rather limiting, if not simplistic. I have been helped by the Jungian approach of Barry Proner, who suggests that the traditional idea of: "whole object relationships being transferred, is outmoded." (Proner, 1997). Proner speaks of part objects being transferred which represent: "early modes of relating" (1997). This is not dissimilar to Angela Molnos' definition:

> Transference is the phenomenon by which patterns of behaviour, responses, the underlying feelings and concomitant anxieties, which have been developed in early childhood, reappear in later relationships, in particular in relation to the therapist and the boundaries of the therapeutic situation itself. [Molnos,1995, p. 33]

The following is an example of how the differing elements of a psychodynamic therapy are often active and intertwined within the sessions and in the relationship between the counsellor and the client.

Jane was sixty. She had been sexually abused by her father as a young girl but it ceased when she was able to challenge him and threaten to expose him (to her mother) if he did not stop. This did not prevent her from marrying a man who turned out to be abusive, both sexually and physically. When she came for counselling she had survived a bitter divorce and was living with her daughter who was now in her late twenties. The daughter treated her mother appallingly. I realized that this behaviour was almost certainly the young woman's projection of the repressed anger she carried towards her father. During the first few sessions I became aware that alongside the storyline of the client something powerful – uncomfortably so – was happening between us, in and beyond the counselling room. Jane periodically showed signs of anger towards me. The anger was not overt but she could hardly contain it. It showed particularly when she had to wait outside the counselling room. On one occasion she had observed a patient leaving and watched the door close behind her. Although it was not time for Jane's appointment and the notice on the door read Counselling, Do not Disturb, Jane knocked on the door, letting me know she was there. I raised this in the session that followed, expressing to Jane my sense of her anger but she was not yet ready to acknowledge it. Jane did not attend the next two sessions. There was no notice given for these absences and no apologies afterwards. After some correspondence a date was agreed for a further session, with a clear understanding that the missed ones could not be retrieved.

The arranged session was painful but positive. In commenting on the missed sessions Jane said that she had "completely forgotten" the first and had confused the time of the other. For a therapist who does not work in a thoroughly psychodynamic way these "explanations" might have been overlooked and disregarded as insignificant. For me they had to be pursued for they might be (and were as it turned out) the patient's way of letting me know something important about how she was feeling and doing so by making me feel as she was feeling. This is of course, at the time, an unconscious process. When I suggested that perhaps her lack of attendance on two consecutive occasions was a thinly disguised expression of anger towards me she was clearly relieved and said how she had been wanting to tell me about her "difficulty with men". She was sufficiently insightful to work out for herself that this rage was triggered in our relationship, though she knew it was some kind of "taking it out on me" and wasn't justified. I told her that I felt she had been letting me know about this anger since we began our sessions and it was good that she could now talk about it openly. I also told her that I had been feeling dominated and pressured by her and that I felt increasingly stuck in trying to help her. This, I suggested to Jane, was her unconscious attempt to put into someone else – in this case the counsellor – her own feelings.

One of the implicit aspects of a psychodynamic understanding, which relates to the above comments, is the powerful influence of the relationship between the counsellor and the client, in the healing process. Certain models of counselling particularly emphasise this point, the best known being *Person or Client-Centred* therapy, which pays great attention to the warmth, empathy and non-judgemental attitude of the therapist. There appears to be good reason to believe that positive results from counselling, whatever the theoretical model used, are more likely to be achieved when the attitude of the therapist and the relationship she or he builds with the client is empathetic and *congruent,* one of the "core condition" words of this therapeutic model, indicating genuineness, both within the counsellor and in the way she/he communicates with the client. This relationship factor needs to be taken fully into account and it is not in fundamental conflict with a psychodynamic approach. I shall certainly draw on some of these concepts later, particularly Rogers' *unconditional, positive regard* as the required attitude of the client-centred counsellor. However, the debate, which would be inappropriate to discuss fully here, is complex. It would be unwise to draw the conclusion that because a particular model of therapy emphasises the therapeutic value of making the other feel wanted, valued and respected, there are not other ways of relating or responding. These alternative responses, although seemingly hurtful, critical and lacking in warmth, are carefully honed skills, tried and tested over years of practice, and used with the client's best interests in mind.

An example of the above point, within psychodynamic counselling, might be the counsellor's abstinence, or at the least, "rule of thumb", in not self-disclosing, or sharing personal information with the client. This abstinence can be experienced by the client as a lack of warmth, or an aloofness, whereas it is an important self-imposed boundary which may lead to the client expressing anger, loss, sadness, initially transferred onto the therapist. If the client can talk openly about these feelings it becomes possible for them to be seen for what they are and where they are really coming from. These comments are not intended as a criticism of client-centred counselling but as a cautionary note that truly helping another is not always about making the other feel good, loved, or accepted. These are indeed desirable aims of therapy but they are sometimes achieved in covert ways. If we find ourselves always saying comforting, pleasing things to another, we need to ask ourselves whether we are trying to protect ourselves rather than really help the other.

The scene is now sufficiently set for us to put on the spectacles that have been prepared for viewing our subject. This viewing is not akin to the one eye which looks through the telescope, for the looking is not only, or predominately, about viewing religion through the lens of psychology or visa versa but rather looking through spectacles, or binoculars. These accommodate both eyes at the same time. So now the metaphor changes slightly but significantly; our focus is not first and foremost on psychology, or religion but on life – experience, relationships, community. I am inviting us to view all of this through the two separate lens of psychology and religion. If we have normal, "binocular (or 3D) vision", each eye sees independently and captures a slightly different image of an object from the other. It is only when these independent images combine simultaneously in the brain that a much fuller, more "rounded" or multidimnsional image is seen. This physical process of how we see, with normal, healthy 3D vision, is a useful analogy for the methodology of complementarity, which I am commending throughout these pages. The one-eyed view, through either a religious or psychological lens, will produce a limited, even distorted image but if our inner eyes look through the lens of *both* religion *and* psychology, independently but simultaneously, a rich, rewarding and more real image will be captured. This is what I mean by complementarity.

It so happens that I do not have binocular, 3D vision… but more of that later.

PART III

Examples of Complementarity

CHAPTER SIX

Responding to evil: splitting and projecting

Every human being in every age, whether religious or not, is faced with the reality of destructive experiences and evil forces. Accident, illness, war, persecution, injustice; these and more, constantly remind us that within all the enjoyment that life can offer, we are fragile, vulnerable creatures, whose lives can be devastated or wiped out within seconds. Further more, we are capable of numerous forms of wickedness, and vulnerable to being on the receiving end of such wickedness. In the world and belief system of the religious person there is an added challenge: if I believe in a loving, sovereign God, how do I respond to the presence of these destructive forces?

At this point I am aware of the need to recognize the distinction between the question of why evil exists per se, and the question of how we respond to the presence of evil, and at the same time to recognize the way in which those two questions overlap. To give a satisfactory answer to the first question is considerably more difficult – we might say infinitely so – than to give one to the second. The different nature of the two questions does not mean that we cannot and should not ask why evil exists but the second question is more urgent and pragmatic; our response to evil will have a profound effect on the way we live our lives and how our living affects others, negatively or positively. It is virtually impossible however to say anything meaningful about the reality of evil and the way we might respond to it, without giving some attention to the question of why evil exists and in the following comments I will not attempt to make a rigid distinction between the two. The question of evil needs to be considered theologically but always in a way which enables us to respond to the presence of evil in our world and in our lives. There is a fascinating story in the New Testament which if read imaginatively – we might again say, using a reader-responsive critical approach – demonstrates this point:

> "As he walked along, he saw a man blind from birth. His disciples asked him, "Rabbi, who sinned, this man or his parents, that he was born blind?" Jesus answered, "Neither this man nor his parents sinned; he was born blind so that God's works might be revealed in him. We must work the works of him who sent me while it is day; night is coming when no one can work. As long as I am in the world, I am the light of the world." " [John 9,1-5]

This story sparkles with theological gems and begs to be interpreted with responsible imagination. Leaving aside the gospel writer's familiar method of letting us know that "healing", in the stories of Jesus and their interpretation, is not merely a cure but wholeness (the blind man has his sight restored but the more profound truth is that Jesus is "the light of the world."), we find ourselves witnessing a theological discussion. The scene is almost a situation comedy, of the "sick" genre. The blind man is not a theory, or a statistic but a particular flesh and blood person, close by, who has never been able to see. The disciples are portrayed as falling into the trap of talking theology about him, rather than doing something for him. Jesus on the other hand, does two things in one fell swoop. First he dismisses the popular theory that illness is the direct result of sin. Second, he appears to be saying – if we read the text in a rigidly literal fashion – that the man's affliction is part of a pre-ordained, divine plan, in order that one day he would be healed, not primarily as an act of compassion but "so that God's works might be revealed in him." As well as rejecting a literalistic handling of the text of the Bible, I would venture the interpretation that the thrust of this story, at this point, is that speculation about the man's illness will not help him; what is needed is a compassionate and practical response. This does not negate the value of theological debate concerning the existence and problem of evil but this debate can only be of use if it enables us to respond positively and creatively in face of evil.

One of the classic ways in which various religions have sought to understand and respond to the presence of evil is the debate about whether evil has a quite separate source from an omnipotent, loving God, or whether this loving God in some paradoxical way is ultimately responsible for evil. The latter part of this alternative is necessary for any monotheistic religion, since an acceptance of an original source of evil, destroys the idea of the sovereignty of God. The attempt to definitively answer the question by postulating two original and separate ultimate powers, namely, God and Satan, (or Light and Darkness, Goodness and Evil, Order and Chaos) is known as Dualism. In his Dictionary, Cross lists three main uses of this term. Clearly, the one which concerns us here is defined as: "A metaphysical system which holds that good and evil are the outcome or product of separate and equally ultimate first causes" (Cross, 1966, p. 424).

It is commonplace to refer to the Judaeo-Christian tradition (particularly if one gives allegiance to either!) as *the* example of how a resort to Dualism has been resisted. It should, however, be acknowledged that other religious traditions have sought to do the same, notably Islam.

In his mammoth work, *Revelation, Rationality, Knowledge and Truth*, the late Mirza Tahir Ahmad, (former Supreme Head of the world-wide Ahmadiyya Muslim Community), whilst acknowledging the "noteworthy contribution" of Zoroastrianism, describes it as a dualistic religion:

> ...not only are truth and goodness eternal, but falsehood and evil also share eternity with them. Both have separate gods who have their own independent orders of management. There is a god of goodness... also known as the god of light and there is a god of evil...also known as the god of darkness; each has his own well-defined role to play. All activity within the universe results from the collision and interaction of these two combatant gods, who are eternally locked in a grim battle of survival and supremacy...Thus Zoroastrian philosophy presents a simple explanation for the coexistence of evil and suffering, goodness and happiness, by attributing their origin to two different sources. [Ahmad, 1998, p. 171]

I have quoted Ahmad extensively for two reasons: first, his description of dualism is noteworthy for its clarity and second, it is part of his argument for setting out his non-dualistic view of Islam. Concluding his refutation of Zoroastrian dualism, he writes: "Dualism when examined in depth is found to be absolutely inadequate in solving the mystery of suffering..." (*ibid.*, p. 177).

His assertion of a non-dualistic view of Islam is every bit as rigorous as one would expect from within Jewish or Christian apologetics. It also, we may note, has a significant resemblance to Jungian psychology:

> Let us remind the reader that Islam defines evil only as a shadow created by the lack of light. It is not a positive existence in itself. We can imagine a source of light (a lamp or the sun), but we cannot imagine any object as a source of darkness. The only way in which an object becomes a source of darkness is through its ability to obstruct light. Likewise, it is only the absence of goodness that constitutes evil. The grades of evil are only determined by the opacity of the obstructing medium. [*ibid.*, p. 193]

I am aware, in quoting Mirza Tahir Ahmad, that he and the Islamic movement he represents are dismissed by what is normally recognized as the voice of traditional Islam but I am not concerned in this context with sectarian conflicts but rather with the way in which the author defends and describes his alternative to dualism. There is, in the case of the theological issue I am exploring no major discrepancy between "traditional" or mainstream Islam and the Ahmadiyya Muslim Community. Both religious movements are monotheistic and therefore both refute dualism.

There are, it seems to me, two major concerns that need to be given some thought before going on to look at the belief in contemporary personifications of evil, which if not always identical with dualism, seek in practice to solve the problem of evil by locating it "outside" God.

The first of these two concerns is to ask whether ancient Judaism, which is the parent of monotheistic religion, does in fact reject dualism as comprehensibly as some of us have thought, or been led to believe. Contemporary scholarship suggests that the picture is not straightforward or conclusive; that it would be simplistic, to say the least, to view the dilemma as an either/or choice between dualism and a God (or more precisely, Yahweh) who is somehow responsible for evil as well as for good, and integrates both . It may well be, as is the case with other theological developments over a long period of time, that the reality is far more varied, fragmented and conflictual. Walter Brueggemann's contributions are particularly noteworthy here. He examines closely and with appreciation, the work of Jon Levenson (Levenson, 1988), in which Levenson argues for a recognizable, and even an established, dualism within the theology of Israel. Brueggemann is not finally persuaded by Levenson's case but that does not prevent him from acknowledging that dualistic beliefs clearly existed in Israel's faith communities. Levenson's argument is found specifically in what he calls "Dualism-in-Creation". Brueggemann states that it is possible to support, on the basis of certain texts, what amounts to: "a primordial dualism in which Yahweh has the upper hand but is not fully in control, and so from time to time creation is threatened." (Brueggemann, 1997, p. 534). He goes on to say: "The clearest exposition of this dualism-in-creation is in Jon Levenson's book..." (ibid., p. 535).

It would be a massive task and fortunately, in the context of my pursuit, an unnecessary one, to rehearse Levenson's argument, or Brueggemann's rejection of its conclusion. The crucial point is that Brueggemann (despite his conclusion), seriously challenges any pre-conceived ideas that dualism was not a facet of the life and theology of ancient Israel:

> "It is my estimate, informed as I am especially by Levenson...that to disregard these texts and their theological counterclaim is impossible on the basis of the texts; moreover, such disregard loses important theological-pastoral resources." [ibid., p. 536]

Brueggemann has done us a great service by drawing us away from any kind of simplistic division of a dualistic or non-dualistic view of Israel's theodicy. He leaves us with a view that not only does justice to a comprehensive survey of the textual evidence but also one which appeals to the social and pastoral realities of Israel's life:

> "The world of blessing under the settled rule of Yahweh is a major affirmation of Israel's testimony. This affirmation would suggest that trust in the world and its generosity is a settled given in Israel's faith and in Israel's experience. We have come by now to expect, however, that any such settled theological claim in Israel is sure to be unsettled, both by experience, which Israel refused to deny, and by texts, which testify to that experience...So it is with Israel's sense of creation. Israel bears witness to the awareness that there is alive in the world a force that is counter to the world of Yahweh, a force that seeks to negate and nullify the world as a secure place of blessing." [ibid., p. 534]

With the benefit of Brueggemann, we are left with what seems to me to be a commonsense picture of God and evil, underpinned by careful textual and theological considerations: like all generations of believers, the people of Yahweh struggled with the immense reality of the presence of evil in God's world. There was, inevitably, a range of views and therefore we find an on-going process of struggle between dualistic and non-dualistic positions. It is the *struggle* that is a characteristic of monotheistic religion, not the supposed fact that a *choice* was made, somewhere along the line, to adopt a non-dualistic view.

I said there were two major concerns that need to be addressed before proceeding. The second is that, if dualism (whether in ancient Israel or in present day faith communities) is at one end of the theological spectrum, how do we respond to the other end, in which God's sovereignty is defended by acknowledging that evil is somehow contained within holiness? In some ways this view is attractive, allowing us to imagine within God a "shadow" side, or aspects of God's nature which resonate with ours, like anger, jealousy, or the need to punish. Certainly from a psychoanalytical perspective, Jungian theories, particularly the idea of the "shadow side" – Jung's term for the primitive, instinctual aspect of human nature and creation – immediately spring to mind. But I am increasingly convinced that simply to leave the case for a non-dualistic position there, is not satisfactory; after all, what does it actually mean to speak of an angry, jealous, or punishing God? How does this work out in our attempt to live a faith-led, faith-inspired life, in our personal relationships and in society and most pointedly, how does it help those who suffer daily and ask, Why me? I am not proposing to attempt an answer to all these important questions but in the next chapter, I will make a serious attempt to say something about whether and in what way our understanding and experience of God justifies using human terms like "anger" to describe God's nature. For the remainder of this chapter we look briefly at the modern religious belief which continues to attribute evil to a being or beings, distinct from God.

I have always found belief in the reality of the "Devil" or "Satan" unnecessary and unacceptable. Such a belief is commonly defended on two grounds. First, by referring to New Testament stories which include references to demons, the Devil, or most frequently, Satan (used as a proper name), especially where such references are attributed to Jesus. The proper name, Satan, is used 35 times in the

New Testament and it is important to note that in all instances: "he is thought of as subordinate to the God who does evil as well as good…" (Richardson, 1957, p. 17).

This meaning of (The) "Satan" makes clear that strictly speaking, belief in Satan, the devil, or demons, does not necessarily constitute dualism, since Satan is not portrayed as God's equal but as God's servant, given the specific task of bringing accusations against God's enemies. Moreover, even with the existence of Satan, the ambivalence is retained, for Yahweh, as Richardson reminds us, *does evil as well as good* (*ibid.*, p. 17). As an example of the latter, Richardson points to Isaiah 45,7:

"I form light and create darkness,
I make weal and create woe;
I the Lord do all these things."

The second ground on which contemporary belief in Satan, or the Devil, is defended is by reference to the personal experience of the believer, who claims to have witnessed both demon-possession and the exorcism of demons.

The first of the above defences results directly from a literalistic handling of the Bible, in which everything (or at least everything the reader chooses) is deemed to mean what it literally says. Often combined with this is the anachronistic view which refuses to accept that although belief in demons and the Devil was real enough in the ancient world, such a belief no longer makes sense in the modern, scientific world. This anachronistic view disregards our modern-day knowledge (albeit limited) of personality, medicine, psychiatry and psychology.

The second of the defences – that of personal experience – rests purely on the interpretation made by the subject. I recall some tense moments in the cell of a top security prison, (when serving as a prison chaplain), in which I was asked to assist a chaplaincy colleague who was ministering to an inmate who appeared to believe that he was "possessed" by demons. After much prayer and perspiration (it took two burly prison officers to restrain the man), the prisoner's agitation subsided. Some days later I asked my colleague, "Do you believe he was possessed by demons?" The chaplain replied, "I'm pretty sure *he* did and if by going along with his belief I can help him, I'm prepared to do it."

I do not wish to go too deeply into arguments for or against objective, personified forms of evil. My purpose in referring to them in this context is to make the point that belief in "the Devil" (and in demons) is neither identical with, nor unrelated to, dualism.

Although the concept of Satan developed into a more powerful and singular figure, "the supernatural adversary *par excellence*" (Richardson, 1957, p. 17), he was always kept in his place, theologically speaking. This constraint is an indication of Jewish and later, Christian belief, to affirm the oneness and supremacy of the divine Being. The latter is maintained in the face of dualism by attributing the more disturbing aspects of human experience to the one God.

I wrote above that whilst personifications of evil are not identical with dualism they are not unrelated. Having tried to support the former statement. I will now turn to the latter.

In some ways it is obvious that the objectification of evil can lead to a dualistic philosophy. Belief in the Devil or demons becomes a transitional stage between understanding evil as integral to God, creation and creatures, and a belief in a separate source of evil, in the form of a particular being. The process is one of an increasing externalisation, distancing and objectifying. It is interesting to note, in this context, that in the critique of Zoroastrianism referred to earlier, the writer claims that Zoroaster himself was not dualistic but that his understanding of evil became misunderstood:

> One can safely deduce from an in-depth study of Zoroastrianism that what was later referred to as an independent God of darkness, was only identical to the concept of a devil found in traditional religions like Judaism, Christianity and Islam. It seems that at some stage the followers of Zoroaster began to misunderstand his philosophy of good and evil, and took them to be the manifestation of two independent, conscious supreme beings who coexisted eternally. [Ahmad, 1998, p. 171]

This then is a good case in point of how "the Devil" was soon assumed to be an entirely separate source of evil.

Although belief in the personification of evil and in Satan or the Devil, as an objective reality – a person – may have been understandable for those living in a pre-scientific world, I wish to argue that this belief is no longer inevitable or appropriate. We need to ask, therefore, why it is so prevalent, not only in what might be loosely termed "folk-lore religion" but as a theological necessity, certainly within most contemporary forms of fundamentalism but also "taken as read" in much evangelical Christianity.

The answer to the above question, from a theological and biblical perspective, is relatively straightforward; it obviously derives from a literalistic handling of scriptural texts. Such an answer takes us so far in our understanding and invites its own examination of why certain believers (of different religions) adhere to biblical literalism. The psychologically curious will, however, wish to look further, at the psychodynamic processes behind the objectification of evil, in particular. Although such contemporary beliefs may not lead to dualism, they are, I suggest, on the same continuum and are therefore driven by the same need; particularly so, if I am correct in arguing that such beliefs are no longer inevitable or appropriate. If it was the case in ancient Israel that a cluster of differing views were held about the presence of evil, including no doubt (and this is where Levenson's study is to be given a fair hearing) dualistic views, we should not be surprised that such views are still held. Regarding both the ancient and the modern world, there is need to recognize that not all believers hold a carefully considered, theologically-honed view on the subject.

By postulating a being called Satan or the Devil, the believer can appear to be no longer impaled on the horns of a familiar dilemma: How can God be supreme and totally in authority over his creation and creatures, when evil, sin or wickedness is so prevalent? The creation – by the believer – of an objective being, called the Devil or Satan, might give the appearance of tidying up the situation nicely; God can now be responsible for goodness, truth and justice, whilst the Devil can take responsibility for the antithesis of these virtues: evil, falsehood and injustice. For the fundamentalist and for many evangelicals, God can still be allowed to mete out punishment and even to cast his creatures into the eternal flames of hell, for such attributes and actions are regarded not as "evil" but as just and necessary.

Dualism, we may conclude, was not and is not, unknown to the Judaeo-Christian, tradition but we follow Brueggemann in asserting that it did not prevail. Contemporary beliefs in a personification of evil, (whether strictly theologically dualistic or not) are neither necessary nor appropriate and are effectively driven by the same desire to account for evil, thereby seeming to preserve the sovereignty of God. On the other hand the temptation to resort to dualism, the struggle to resist it and the resulting ambivalence which the believer holds – all these *are* authentic to the Judaeo-Christian tradition.

I have tried to represent in the argument above a picture of what is crucial for any religious understanding of evil; crucial most of all, because anything less than a rejection of dualism effectively avoids the problem of evil and the existential realities which people face.

In Michael Jacob's excellent book, *Living Illusions: A Psychology of Belief*, he finds space to devote several paragraphs on the subject of the relationship between good and evil, the psychological process of *splitting* and its theological counterpart in dualistic belief. Jacobs finds himself, without using my terminology, applying a complementarity approach which leads naturally to the following comparison:

> Here, in psychological form, is one of the most taxing of all theological questions. How can a good God (like a good mother) allow bad things to happen? Splitting is seen in faith terms wherever there is dualistic belief – the belief in two gods, one of whom is good and the other of whom is evil. [Jacobs, 1993, p. 79]

It is interesting and important to notice Jacob's careful use of language; the comparison is between a good mother who is experienced alternatively as good and bad. That is to say, the reality of the child's experience is that mother acts in a contradictory way but the wider reality is that she is a *good* mother. Because of the careful language, the comparison is sustainable and borne out even in the way the question is phrased: *How can a good God... allow bad things to happen?* This is seriously different from, *How can a good God do bad things?*

Living with this "unknowing", suffering the apparent absence, indifference, or injustice of God, is essential to faith but it does not lead me to the conclusion that God – Being itself – has spiteful, vengeful, or punishing attributes.

The debate in hand becomes even more teasing when attitudes and actions which some people of faith interpret as good, in the sense of just or righteous, are considered bad to the point of being barbaric and cruel by others. When, for example, a worshipper sings, in a traditional Harvest Festival Service, the rousing words, "Come, ye thankful people, come..." does he or she retain the aura of joy and gladness when voicing these lines of the penultimate verse?

For the Lord our God shall come,
And shall take his harvest home;
From his field shall in that day
All offences purge away;
Give his angels charge at last
In the fire the tares to cast,
But the fruitful ears to store
In his garner evermore.
(*Hymns and Psalms*, 1983, n. 355, v. 3, Henry Alford (1810—71)

Does she or he sing these words at all and if so, what does that say about the God being worshipped, the worshipper and the people who (if you will forgive the pun), "draw the short straw"? It seems to me much more obvious and understandable to suspect that in the case of punishment and eternal damnation, we human beings impose our own needs to punish onto God. In this sense Freud may not have been entirely wrong. However, whilst Freud is correct to reject the human-shaped God which we are so prone to make, he is not interested in entertaining the idea that there might be faith in God which is not so susceptible to the criticism of projection.

I think a strong convergence occurs at this point between religion and psychology and that the psychological element of this convergence is to be found in a process looked at in Chapter 5, the process of *transference*. Transference is an important tool for the therapist and for this reason and because of the implications that an understanding of transference has for the theme of this chapter, I will devote what may at first seem like a disproportionate amount of time to exploring and illustrating its meaning further.

Many psychodynamic counsellors regard what is usually termed *working in the transference* as the most important part of the therapeutic process. Underlying or within the problems which clients present when seeking counselling there are frequently relationship difficulties, which invariably have their origins in *transference*. That is to say, an internalized feeling from the past, associated with a particular person, or aspect of a person, becomes transferred onto a person, or several people, in the present, causing considerable distortions and damaging effects, in personal, family and work-colleague relationships. The counsellor will certainly talk with the client about how this is happening and this is frequently received as either a powerful and helpful insight, or an elucidation and affirmation of what the client already feels or senses but has not fully understood. However, the most effective way to use transference is not by talking about it but by working *in* the transference. The counsellor (though not usually the client) is aware of and sensitive to the transference that is already present and active in the room. If the counsellor can allow these transference feelings to be expressed by the client, there will soon enough be an opportunity for this in-the-room transference to be talked about with the client.

It is perhaps best if I attempt to illustrate the above, in general terms, by asking you to imagine a client who carries unresolved feelings of anger and fear, originating in her relationship with a strict, judgemental father. The counsellor may be experienced by the client, not only as a professional carer, with training and knowledge in a particular field but as an authoritative, parental figure who wields power and who may use this power to judge and criticise her. The client begins, in other words, to imagine the counsellor *as if* he were her father; the residual feelings of fear and anger which originated in her relationship with her father are now evoked and felt towards the counsellor. It is as though a nerve has been touched inside the client. More accurately, it is a psychological, emotional wound that has been touched and which is crying out to be acknowledged and healed. The reason why this unresolved pain and accompanying, unheard voice, directs itself at the therapist is because, initially at least, it will always seek to find a resolution by avoiding the real place of pain.

I clearly remember, in the early days of my training, when the significance and power of transference was still confusing and rather frightening to me, making a venture into the transference arena. I had been counselling a young woman, for several sessions, whose circumstances were not unlike the ones in the above generalized illustration. The abusive experience she had of her father had been repeated in subsequent relations with men. Thankfully, she expressed feeling safe and not too uncomfortable in the counselling, at which point I risked asking what feelings she had had, or thoughts she had entertained, when the counselling began, especially as I was a man and old enough to be her father. Her reply shocked me and taught me an important lesson about the power of transference feelings. She answered as though relieved to be asked and to have the opportunity to tell me: "O, even before our sessions began, I had fears that you would criticise me." She hesitated and added, "I even thought that you might hit me." When she saw the pained and puzzled look on my face, she struggled to explain: "I know it sounds silly... I don't mean I really thought you would hit me...I know you wouldn't...but it felt like that."

The colossal therapeutic value of using the transference of the counselling relationship is that it can be acknowledged and used to help the client be more aware of the source of the real pain and loss involved in past experience and relationships. When this occurs, a delayed mourning process can begin and positive changes can begin to take place in her or his life and relationships.

Transference then is a powerful, largely unconscious process, which affects all of us in varying ways and with varying degrees of intensity. It is always evoked in relationships since that is where the attached feeling would have originated. Transference, damaging and destructive as it may be on occasions, is one of the ways in which we manage our relationships and cope with life. It is strongly operative in "falling in love" and when we make unconscious choices regarding a partner or friend. It is part of our internal "mapping" system, which instinctively puts us on our guard when we meet a perceived danger. The drawback of transference is that its unconscious process bypasses our conscious, adult, reflective self. That is why making transference feelings conscious is an important step forward, whether inside or beyond the counselling room.

Since our use of the term "God" refers to a reality who is profoundly mysterious – One who encompasses us but whom we cannot get our minds around – it is inevitable that we *transfer* our human experience, shaped by our upbringing and environment, onto God. I remember learning this lesson, without being critically aware of the psychological process involved, or the psychodynamic meaning of the word *transference*. I was a young Minister at the time, in only my second appointment. We had a Sunday night youth group, which a handful of young teenagers attended, mostly children of regular church members, plus one or two friends of friends, who drifted in from time to time. I recall talking about the Prodigal Son and how the father in the parable acted as a good father would, in welcoming home his wayward son with generous, unconditional love. This love, I went on to say, typified the love of God, our heavenly Father. At some point in this vain exercise of attempting to say something meaningful and convincing, I was quite rudely brought down to earth by one of the "drifters". His sudden heart-felt outburst was without doubt the most important lesson of the evening: "If God's like my fucking father, I don't want to know him; I've not even seen him for five years!"

Of course I realize now that I mishandled the interpretation of the famous parable by drawing a picture of a "good enough" earthly, human father and comparing this with the "heavenly Father" who was like so but infinitely more so. Instead, I should have turned the whole thing on its head and begun with the picture of the Heavenly Father portrayed in the prodigal's father, which of course was alien to the hurt and angry young teenager. But this "lesson" wasn't about biblical interpretation but the profoundly damaging effect negative hurtful relationships can have, especially when experienced in childhood and how those experience become the raw material for later "transferences".

In this chapter I have begun to explore some of the problems which the presence of evil poses, not only for the philosophy of religion but for the person of faith. I have noted in particular how communities of faith throughout the history of religion have struggled to maintain an integrated understanding of God and how this has required a refutation of dualism. There is however a debate beyond this debate, so to speak, for if dualism if to be refuted how is faith in a sovereign God to be shaped? How do we understand and believe in a God of love who is responsible for good and evil? In exploring these major themes my main aim will be to bring to light the psychological and theological complementarity which will strengthen and commend the arguments offered.

CHAPTER SEVEN

Responding to evil: integration and ambivalence

In Chapter 8, I shall look more closely at some questions around sin and salvation which will resonate with points touched on in this chapter. For the present, I shall pursue the question raised in the previous chapter of whether we can make sense of a God who is ultimately responsible for evil as well as good.

If a dualistic view is not an acceptable theological response to the problem of evil, how do we respond to the further question of believing in a God who not only knows of evil and is obviously responsible for allowing it to occur but who also appears to act, on occasions, in evil, contradictory and vengeful ways? To put the question somewhat differently, "Are we content to think and speak of the God we might place our faith in as one who acts with anger or jealousy, who at times chooses to punish people and who casts those who refuse to acknowledge him into the eternal flames of hell?" I have deliberately slipped in the words "anger" and "jealousy", since it is fair to say that they are frequently included in contemporary discussions of those characteristics which might be seen or experienced as, at best, a bewildering and dark side of God or, at worst, a seemingly evil side. Of course it is relatively easy for blood and thunder passages, especially in the Old Testament, to be understood as the best way in which people of an ancient faith could make sense of life and then for such passages to be dismissed as having no contemporary value. That argument holds good only so far and then begins to feel suspiciously as though it is dodging important questions. It would be to misjudge and discredit those ancient people of faith simply to disregard these uncomfortable aspects of God's nature. These ancients are conveying their experience of God and it needs to be taken seriously and reinterpreted rather than dismissed. However, I am left with a feeling that there are many serious contemporary attempts to avoid a dualistic view of God which fail to come to grips with such a reinterpretation and therefore leave the problem unresolved.

The use of language here is of utmost importance and this is particularly so regarding the word anger. Our human experience of anger is so powerful and often enormously difficult to understand, to express, or to manage, that to attribute anger to God will result in compounding this confusion. Convergence and complementarity presents itself powerfully and inescapably at this point since psychodynamic therapy (as well as certain other counselling models) regards the experience and understanding of human anger as of great importance. At first glance, anger hardly appears to be a likely candidate for convergence and complementarity in religion and psychology. In fact, a popular (if misguided) view of religious faith is that for the most part the display of anger is to be avoided and that even to feel or harbour anger is sinful. It is no less than striking that the word anger and its variations, used to describe human emotion, occurs infrequently in the New Testament. My quick scan of a Biblical concordance resulted in only ten instances. Even more significant is the fact that almost all of these instances portray anger as undesirable or downright sinful; the following is not untypical:

> Put away from you all bitterness and wrath and anger and wrangling and slander, together with all malice, and be kind to one another…Therefore be imitators of God…and live in love… [Ephesians 4,31-32; 5,1–2]

Two things immediately strike me in this passage: first, "anger and wrath" are grouped with features of human behaviour which although readily recognised as undesirable, have a quite different, more sinister connotation than "wrath and anger". Secondly, this composite list of evils is contrasted to "kindness" and living "in love". My response to this contrast would not suggest convergence but conflict. Thinking and working psychodynamically has enabled me to see that the opposite to love is not anger but indifference. Where then does anger belong, or from where does it arise? Without attempting to be precise, for precision is not the most helpful way forward here, anger is paradoxically related to love itself; it belongs to passion. It can be said that in making this point, I am clearly disagreeing with the writer of Ephesians and of course that is so. However, it is also true that the Bible itself holds contrasting and conflicting views on many issues and that one text does not always convey that ring of authenticity which is found by wrestling with Scripture as a whole.

Let me evoke a rather different picture of anger, within the same Christian Testament. Of the very few references to human anger I have indicated, only one or two are about the anger of the man Jesus. Of course it is possible to look at similar feelings attributed to Jesus and in a more in-depth study of this point, this would be profitable. For now I will stay with one example (in which the italics are mine):

> Again he entered the synagogue, and a man was there who had a withered hand. They watched him to see whether he would cure him on the sabbath, so that they might accuse him. And he said to the man who had the withered hand, "Come forward." Then he said to them, "Is it lawful to do good or to do harm on the sabbath, to save life or to kill?" But they were silent. He looked around at them with *anger*, he was *grieved* at their hardness of heart and said to the man, "Stretch out your hand." He stretched it out, and his hand was restored. The Pharisees went out and immediately conspired with the Herodians against him, how to destroy him. [Mark 3,1-6]

The observation, within this story, of the response of Jesus to his shamed-faced critics, offers an insight into a refined understanding of what we generally refer to as anger: the comment that Jesus "looked around at them with anger" is immediately qualified with the phrase, "…he was grieved at their hardness of heart…"

If I am now asked whether it is appropriate to say that God can be angry, or whether anger is an aspect of God's nature, I would have to reply "No" – and "Yes". Of course it is not appropriate to say that anger is an aspect of God's nature if by doing so we imagine for one second that we are defining a facet of God's nature that is immediately within our grasp and understanding. But if I am allowed with Michael Jacobs to speak tentatively about "illusions" (of faith), I can say "Yes" without needing to be definitive. In doing so, I am greatly helped by the picture of a passionate God; One who is deeply moved and affected by the impairment or self-destruction of God's own good creation. "Anger", I am now helped to see, is perhaps more like grieving than anger as we so commonly know and express it. In a similar fashion, "jealousy" (when attributed to God) is our straining attempt to describe an aspect of the depth of an indescribable love, who is Being Itself.

The convergence and complementarity arising from the above comments is powerful. In the daily work of counselling, I encounter, like many therapists, the presence of and stories about, repressed anger. Because the anger is repressed it is communicated as unresolved feeling oozing from wounds inflicted long ago; wounds yearning to find healing, whose pain is projected on to others (or turned in on oneself) in a desperate effort to avoid the real cause of the pain. Alongside and interrelated to a deep sense of loss and sadness, this anger lies just below the weight of depression, which so many people are suffering when seeking counselling. This projected anger is not yet the grieving anger of which I have spoken; it moves towards that as the therapeutic process works. At its worst it is usually spiteful, unfair and destructive of the self and of others. This is no light matter for in its extreme forms of projection it can lead to severe abuse in relationships, including suicide and murder. It is this distorted form of anger which falls within the description of Ephesians, quoted above: "wrangling and slander, together with all malice." I hope that now, the confusion and the distinction between the anger which is indeed unhealthy and that which is somehow an indicator of the mystery of God's "anger", is clearer. God's "anger", we must say, is not the result of projection.

Psychodynamic psychology takes anger seriously. It recognises the sickness of repressed, or depressed anger but it also recognises, in a way that religion and the church has not always been able to do, the healthiness of anger being expressed for what it is, accompanied by a proper grieving process. When I look deep into religion, and this is profoundly true when looking at the person of Jesus, the complementarity is so compelling that my faith is strengthened and affirmed and simultaneously, my work as a counsellor,

I am grateful that in shaping the thoughts on the subject of this chapter, I was introduced to two especially thoughtful and thought-provoking recent books, both of which, in their own way, converge with where I have also arrived.

In the first of these two books (Phillips, 2005), Anthony Phillips explores what he refers to throughout as "the shadow side of

God". This is explained variously as God's apparent indifference, absence and even his apparent injustice. The book is challenging and thought-provoking and overall I found it helpful and thought the author courageous in addressing this immense subject in such a real and robust way. The book has the merit of facing realistically the apparent absence of God in the most painful of experiences and of acknowledging that there are times when God seems to treat us unjustly, even to abandon us. This book is clearly a serious and worthy attempt to explore part of the subject I have been looking at but simultaneously it highlights the dilemma we can find ourselves in if we resist a dualistic faith. Phillips is primarily concerned to stay with the reality of how people of faith can sometimes feel, whatever the infinitely wider reality of God's mysterious ways. In other words, it indicates that the author is describing how people of faith experience God, which of course may not be precisely what is going on from God's perspective. As an example of this we might note the experience of the man on a cross who cries "My God, my God, why have you forsaken me?". We have no reason to doubt the integrity of this intensely personal experience. At the same time, retrospectively, the person of faith believes in and points to a wider reality, of a God who is far from absent; in reality a God who suffers within the suffering man. The keeping of this paradoxical tension is expressed by Phillips in his frequent use of the word "apparently" when speaking of our experience of God's injustice, harshness, or betrayal of us. However, there are other occasions when his language appears not to be paradoxical but quite unequivocal.

> "...all must recognize that there may lie in the future an indescribable agony when, abandoned by the very God on whom they had come to rely, they are plunged into the dark abyss where all that has meaning becomes meaningless." [Phillips, 2005, p. 117]

Perhaps it is not intended but Phillip's language, in this passage and in others, lacks a certain "as if" element; it seems that God really does forsake us and that his "shadow side" is harsh, even cruel. The "as if" is not unlike the "as if" of transference in the therapy world.

I was left rather confused after reading the book as to whether the "shadow side of God" is an appropriate phrase to describe what the author is meaning. The phrase, a Jungian one, as we have noted previously, does have an attraction, not least to the psychologically aware but would it not be more accurate to say that the "shadow" is cast by ourselves, as those whose vision is blurred, like those who only "see in a mirror dimly" (1 Cor. 13,12)?

This blurred vision is not necessarily a reference to our "sin" as human beings, but rather the inevitable ignorance, in our time-bound existence, of not knowing. This "not knowing" can understandably be filled with fears and feelings that God has withdrawn and abandoned us; that it is God's anger, punishment, or cruel indifference. The attempts of a mother to give assurance to her child that it is not in the child's best interest to play with the dials on the electric cooker, rarely prevent the infant from reacting as though his mother is wickedly depriving him.

The following extract from Phillips shows how his concern to stay with the real experience of the believer stretches the paradox to its utmost limits but the last phase of the sentence returns to the wider, mysterious reality, that God not only displays love but in all ways and at all times, is love: "By experiencing the bitterness of his shadow side, entering that dark abyss of godforsakenness, we are strangely invited to allow him to realize in us what all along he had intended for us" (Phillips, 2005, p. 117f).

The second of the books (Dawes, 2006) that I look upon as recent "Godsends" is a joyous offering from Stephen Dawes, an Old Testament scholar and practising Methodist Minister. Both scholarly insight and pastoral experience combine as the author explores and pleads for a more positive appreciation of what those of Christian faith disparagingly term the "Old Testament." Psalm 103 is the focus of the author's exploration, which takes us to the heart of the God who is the same yesterday, today and forever. There is much in this book to ponder and I do it little justice by highlighting just one point made. With regard to my immediate concern – to discover and stay with a balanced, paradoxical understanding of God's nature – the author approaches the subject of God's "anger" with no less courage and realness than Phillips. Dawes uses the same metaphor, of the "shadow side", as Phillips, but interestingly, unlike Phillips, he uses it not to describe the puzzling, difficult to digest, aspects of God's nature but of "the shadow side of human life". (Dawes, 2006, p. 33). God's nature, on the other hand, is explored against an all-encompassing backcloth of *Chesed*: "a rich technical term from the theological vocabulary of the Old Testament…" (*ibid.*, p. 25).

It is worth quoting Dawes at some length to catch the flavour of where he is leading us:

> The Old Testament and the New both agree that God exhibits anger and that this anger is directed against evil and at human sin...Sin, in all its chameleon colours, makes God angry because it fouls up his creation and spoils life for its victims. And, surely, in the face of this it would be a poor God who did not get angry?...Only a heartless and unloving God would not. A God who did not get angry would be as useless and as uncaring as a parent who did not care how badly one of their children hurt the others, or how much damage they did to themselves or other people. The picture of a parent is important here, for good parents do get angry, and they get angry because they care. Here the psalmist voices the common view of his faith that God feels anger, just as we do, with all its potent mixture of rage, grief, frustration, hurt and fear, and he does so because he cares. God's anger, then, is not a contradiction of his love, but a sign of it. [*Ibid.*, p. 33f]

This is a splendid affirmation of the mystery of God's love and I am helped in pursuing my own aim, in noticing how in the above quotation the psalmist's "common view of his faith" includes "grief" as an aspect of God's "anger" Dawes leaves us in no doubt that anger is a legitimate way of describing an aspect or expression of God's love but this is very different from a God whose "anger" punishes the "sinner" with various afflictions in this life, or the anger which burns so fiercely that it consigns such sinners to the flames of eternal punishment. It is not in other words a destructive anger but a way of attempting to describe the overflowing and passionate care of God for creation and the grief and sadness when that care is not embraced. Whether it is helpful to use the word "anger" to describe this aspect of God's love, is a mute point, given its many negative and vengeful understandings in human discourse.

I have been concerned throughout these two chapters on evil, and throughout this whole discussion, to make the point that God can best be pictured as one who cannot be known or grasped; holiness is not definable and is not ours to manipulate or contain. The believer is asked to put faith in a generous, *grace-full* God, whose invitation is to realize and incorporate that we are accepted. It is perfectly understandable, when we feel abandoned, even by God, or when we cannot fathom who God is, let alone what God is doing, or when "natural disasters" strike, or loved ones die, for us to fear that we are experiencing the anger and judgement of God and his punishment for our sins. Yet before we rush to attribute to this God the painful episodes of our time-bound experiences, perhaps we should pause and ask whether we are making God in our own image. An alternative would be to live with the unknowing and retain our faith in a God of love, in whose "everlasting arms" we are ultimately safe. To leave behind the god of our creating, is to experience a loss, a bereavement, but those who choose this path often find – as always when we let go of false hope – a release and freedom which brings a new lease of life.

I want to make comment on one more aspect of the subject of understanding God's apparent "shadow side" before leaving the subject of evil.

I have stated that it is crucial, as a person of religious faith, to understand suffering, tragedy and I would add, so-called "natural disasters", without implying, or positively stating, that God has a vengeful, punishing facet to his nature. This argument is, I believe, further strengthened by a more traditional one, the theme of which is totally consistent with a psychodynamic psychology.

I have long been attracted to a theory which centres around the way in which, in the New Testament letters attributed to Paul, the Greek word *orge* (pronounced orgay and translated *wrath* or *anger*) is used. The reader will forgive me (or thank me!) if we avoid a comprehensive survey of this debate. The gist of it is that *orge* is used in two tantalizingly different phrases, which simply translated are, *The wrath of God* and *The wrath*. The debate has focused on the personal and impersonal implications of these phrases. There appears to be little doubt that in both cases of the usage, the letter writer is referring to anger that is the result of neglecting or ignoring God's love and righteousness. I do not think, therefore, that Paul, by using the shorter, impersonal phrase, is attempting to distance *wrath* from God, or to extract it from a theological framework.

Without suggesting that we can know exactly why this difference of expression is used, or what was the intention of the user, there is an interpretation which is supportable and makes much sense: the intransitive use of *orge* helps us to see that wrath is not God's personal angry response to his sinful creatures but the inevitable consequence of ignoring, abusing, or flouting, the way of creation. Of course this "creation" is God's creation but the distinction is now, I hope, a little clearer. Put, once again, in terms of a human family, we would have no difficulty in sensing the difference. Let's picture parents, firmly but gently and with supporting love, encouraging their toddler to explore the home environment but carefully pointing out certain areas or actions as forbidden, because of danger to the child. Let's further suppose that the inevitable happens and the child wilfully disobeys, or much more likely, forgets, and an accident ensues. We would not, I suggest, understand the sore fingers or grazed knee of the child as the parents' punishment; neither, I trust, would we approve of the response, "That will teach you!", or "You've got what you deserve!" Of course there is a learning to be had from such experiences but that is quite different from punishment for sins committed.

Can we accept that we live in a universe where it is necessary for things to hold together and that in human relationships, social life, nature and our environment, behaving irresponsibly, in a careless, avaricious manner, will have inevitable disruptive, damaging, consequences? The consequences model is subtly but profoundly different from that of a God who angrily punishes. To give another very human illustration: it is correct that in certain instances the disease of AIDS may be a consequence of irresponsible sexual behaviour but that is significantly different from saying that aids is a *punishment* for irresponsible sexual behaviour.

Wearing our custom-made spectacles, I now want to ask what might be further points of convergence which offer a real complementarity between religion and psychology in respect of the enormous, age-old problem of evil? If *transference* is a psychodynamic process that can help us to understand the unhealthy aspects of religious faith (and indeed of all distorted and destructive human behaviour), where do we find further complementarity which speaks of a healing process?

Klein's point, discussed earlier, that the psychological process, experienced by human beings, of moving from the *paranoid-schizoid position* to the *depressive position "to some extent applies to the whole of life"* gives us a clue. Klein also believed that, even as adults, we can never entirely work through the depressive position (which would mean a perfectly integrated life) and that we occupy the depressive position (a more realistic "place" than the paranoid-schizoid position) to a lesser or greater degree, depending on our experience of childhood and subsequent experiences. During times of particular stress and vulnerability, we can each revert to the paranoid-schizoid position.

I have said earlier that in Klein's model, the infant introjects and processes her or his experience before projecting it. In the early, paranoid-schizoid position, the infant is too emotionally immature to cope with the ambivalence of good and bad and defends himself/herself against the threat of this happening by splitting these aspects before projecting one or the other. The insecure adult (or the one who is feeling vulnerable or threatened) will act in a similar way. Evidence of this is not hard to find at all levels of human relationship. It may be a politician who labels all the occupants of a particular race or nation as "the enemy", implying that, without exception, they each have evil intents. Political leadership of the United States during the 1980s was inclined to see all Russians as "the enemy" – the antipathy of the assumed ideal of the American way of life and its godly principles. Few of us who experienced that era were not tainted by that projection and its image of "reds under the beds". More recently, similar concerns have been expressed about American foreign policy in Iraq, and its counterpart in the United Kingdom. "Ethnic Cleansing" in recent and current history is a further chilling example of the deadly consequences of how as adults we *act out* from a *paranoid/schizoid "position"*.

What happens, in varying degrees, at a national, political and institutional level, happens constantly in inter-personal relationships. Accusative generalisations, which often begin with words like, "they" or "them" are often projections, which allow us to distance, objectify and simplify the challenges of real and healthy relationships, which require an insight into and an acceptance of the composite nature of both, groups of people, and of each individual.

Projection (in its negative form) is the psychological mechanism we use to condemn fellow human beings. The alternative – that we assess each person individually – is not only emotionally demanding but will involve us accepting undesirable aspects of ourselves that we recognise in the other. This unacceptable part of ourselves is conveniently split off and projected on to the other, as a person or as a group. Within families or other social groups, we are all guilty of "taking out" on another an unpleasant experience that has little or nothing to do with the other. This "displacement" (a form of projection) is far more widespread than we often recognise or are willing to accept and has serious consequences, manifested in many kinds of physical, verbal, sexual and emotional abuse.

I want now to follow Klein's theory through to indicate how the movement from unhealthy to healthy religion takes place.

As with Klein's two *paranoid/schizoid* and *depressive positions*, there can be no absolutes in terms of religious development; we are each part of a process and we each vacillate between maturity and immaturity in our spirituality. In a picture of healthiness, we would expect to find as little "splitting" as possible and therefore a corresponding minimum degree of projection. This in turn would be reflected in a spirituality in which God would be experienced and regarded, not as a clearly definable being, whose will can be readily deduced (as long as sufficient faith and prayer is offered) but as inscrutable, indefinable, mysterious and unfathomable.

Within the "mature" picture would be an acceptance that there is a strong paradoxical feel about God, Being itself, or Holiness. I favour the word "Holiness" as an alternative to "Being Itself" since it is more indicative of the believer's sense of the personal nature, as well as the awe and wonder, of God's presence. The nature of this presence is located in vulnerability and unconditional loving-care, as depicted, for example, by the man Jesus. In this view there would be no attempt to locate God; God would be no more up there than down here. In fact what I have called the "mature" picture finds much support in the Biblical tradition. Jesus is portrayed teaching his disciples that the *Kingdom of God* (God's presence or reign) is not locatable:

> Once Jesus was asked by the Pharisees when the kingdom of God was coming, and he answered, ""The kingdom of God is not coming with things that can be observed; nor will they say, "Look, here it is!" or "There it is!" For, in fact, the kingdom of God is among you." [Luke 17,20–21]

The elusive nature of Holiness is by no means exclusive to the New Testament but has powerful precedents throughout the Bible. When Moses seeks authority as Yahweh's messenger he receives an elusive response:

> But Moses said to God, "If I come to the Israelites and say to them, "The God of your ancestors has sent me to you", and they ask me, "What is his name?" what shall I say to them?" God said to Moses, "I am who I am."

He said further, "Thus you shall say to the Israelites, "I am has sent me to you." [Exodus 3,13-14]

Similarly, when the patriarch, Jacob requests the name (effectively, the identity) of the river god he struggles with by the brook Jabbok, at Peniel, his request is refused but he is nevertheless blessed:

Then Jacob asked him, "Please tell me your name." But he said, "Why is it that you ask my name?" And there he blessed him. [Genesis 32,29]

When Moses asks Yahweh to show him his glory, the request is granted but in an ambivalent way, in which Moses is given a tantalizing back-view of God; one which is nevertheless appropriate for a relationship of faith:

The LORD said to Moses, "I will do the very thing that you have asked; for you have found favour in my sight, and I know you by name." Moses said, "Show me your glory, I pray." And he said, "I will make all my goodness pass before you, and will proclaim before you the name, "The LORD"; and I will be gracious to whom I will be gracious, and will show mercy on whom I will show mercy. But", he said, "you cannot see my face; for no one shall see me and live." And the LORD continued, "See, there is a place by me where you shall stand on the rock; and while my glory passes by I will put you in a cleft of the rock, and I will cover you with my hand until I have passed by; then I will take away my hand, and you shall see my back; but my face shall not be seen." [Exodus 33,17-23]

This picture of "mature faith" which I have tried to draw, corresponds to the Depressive Position in Klein's model of the human psyche, representing a phase of development in which the ambivalent nature of life – not least of human beings – is struggled with and begins to be accepted. This would be reflected in how the believer used the symbols and signs of religion, whether graphic and linguistic representations, or those religious stories that we call myths. Mature faith would use them as transitory indicators, pointing beyond themselves to that which is beyond definition and can only be glimpsed or alluded to.

The emphasis in this book is not to summarize the various attempts which describe a psychology of faith but to point to the complementarity between certain understandings of faith and a psychodynamic understanding of human nature, so that one may shed light on the other. I am attempting to point to an element in the wider debate of the psychology of religion which I hope others might develop. Unless such a quest is pursued, attempts to describe faith in terms of its maturity or development face the criticism of being value judgements. We cannot, of course, avoid making such judgements but an attempt at complementarity, or correspondence, offers a more holistic view and strengthens the integrity of the argument. If Klein is anywhere near right in suggesting that, in emotional and psychological terms, a person is more developed, more healthy, or (as Jungians might say) more individuated, when struggling with and attempting to work through the *depressive position* rather than being stuck in the *paranoid/schizoid position* this would help to validate those expressions of faith which embrace those psychological elements.

CHAPTER EIGHT

The self, salvation and unconditional positive regard

Sermon illustrations are a powerful means of communication when they do the job well; used naively they can be seriously misleading. The preacher began his "Children's Address" in an arresting fashion. Without a word, he set in motion a vacuum cleaner (which lay conveniently close to hand.) He told the children, and reminded the older generation of adults, of an early television advert in which a door-to-door salesman was allowed, by an alarmingly obliging housewife, to decorate her hitherto clean carpet with a variety of pre-packaged dirt. This dirt was then comprehensively despatched by the cleaner which, some may remember, "beats as it sweeps as it cleans".

My worst fears were realised in the preacher's interpretation: as with the sweeper, so with Jesus our Saviour; he sucks up the entire "dirt" (sins) in our lives. End of message. Of course the fact that the lady's carpet would probably never experience such a severe soiling and that the all-powerful "hoover" was needed only because the salesman had introduced the dirt in the first place, was conveniently overlooked. However, it provided me with a picture of much preaching and theology, which effectively sabotages the radically startling and often offensive thrust of the ministry and teaching of Jesus, as he is encountered in the Christian testament.

Christian religion has all too often introduced sin into people's lives in order to convince them of the need for a saviour. Any religion which is founded on a saviour figure is prone to the temptation of promoting the idea that human beings are shot through with sin, from which they need to be saved. Pruyser, recognising the positive contribution of Freud's critique of religion, makes a similar point:

...I would hold that religion is, psychologically, something like a rescue operation, whatever other functions it may have or whatever it may be in essence. It is born from situations in which someone cries "Help!" The Salvation Army and the so-called evangelical groups know this, and the Psalmist gave it poetic expression in words that can move hearts of stone. [Pruyser, 1971, p. 25f]

And later: "Apart from religion's astoundingly diverse traditions and institutional trappings, its rescue motif alone is enough to make it forever popular. But therein lies its gravest danger..." (Pruyser, 1977a, p. 49).

I am not suggesting that the Christian doctrine of salvation (from sin) is entirely invalid but that it becomes formulated in a particular way because of an assumption that the *focus* of Christ's saving work is to rescue individuals *from* something and the further assumption that "sin" is the something. Addressing the subject of *"Narcissistic motives in Historical Religiosity"* Pruyser writes:

Scores of people labor under the conviction that they must be saved – saved from something untoward or nasty, and saved unto something desirable. This grand theme, which runs through several of the world's major religions, is at times appropriated in blatantly narcissistic ways, namely when it takes the form of a proprietary concern over one's own soul to the utter neglect of redemption of communities, nations or mankind at large. [Pruyser, 1978, p. 68]

The pictures we have in the canonical Gospels, although historically scanty, yield sufficient to suggest a rather different understanding of Jesus as saviour from the traditional concept of salvation *from sin*. The image which comes to mind is one of saving that which is *already present*; preserving, cherishing and nurturing what is good, so that it does not become diminished, undervalued or ultimately lost. The words you are now reading were preserved on my computer a few moments after typing them, by pressing the "save" command. There is also the option, when saving material on a computer, to "save as"; for example, a particular file format. Without, I hope, straining the analogy, this might serve to emphasise the positive nature of salvation in which it is *for* or *to* something, rather than *from* something. Of course, it is true that the corollary of this is that what is being saved is saved from something; to be more precise, it is being saved from being lost, from alienation and ultimately from going out of being. Perhaps we should remember also that what is "written off" and apparently lost forever, on a computer, is often retrievable.

What evidence is there in the historical ministry of Jesus, pictured in the Gospels, to support the idea of salvation as primarily a valuing and enhancing of what is good rather than a rescuing from what is bad? The evidence, in the form of an emphasis, is clear and consistent. Looking at how Jesus is portrayed relating to people, we might take, by way of an example, the story of Zacchaeus (Luke 19,1-10). If we are to take Zacchaeus as typical of his kind, he would most certainly have been "written off" and considered lost (outside the pale of the covenant people of Israel) by the respectable of his day. This story serves as a good example, not least because it offers a description or model of "salvation":

> Then Jesus said to him, "Today Salvation has come to this house, because he too is a son of Abraham. For the Son of man came to seek out and to save the lost." [Luke 19,9f]

Why is it, in the Zacchaeus story, that Jesus is portrayed as joyously affirming salvation for this man? The dynamics of the story are striking and relate to the sequence in which the "salvation" takes place. We notice first that Zacchaeus is not asked to "repent" of his sins (of which he undoubtedly had many). Neither does the story tell us that Jesus made any mention of these sins; rather, it tells of Jesus inviting himself to a meal in the man's home. This self-invite can be taken, not as audacity but as a sign of acceptance, since table fellowship was regarded (and still is) amongst Jewish people, as a relationship of intimacy, welcome and inclusiveness. The fact that it is the guest rather than the host who makes the invitation does nothing to weaken this point; according to the story we may assume that Zacchaeus felt honoured to be the host. We might also say, without any sense of triteness, that Jesus showed this money-grubbing Jewish quisling *unconditional positive regard*. It was *unconditional* in that Jesus required nothing of the man at this point, except to be a host. It was certainly *positive* in as much as the "sins" of Zacchaeus, though presumably not unknown to Jesus, were over-looked and consequently he was *regarded*, not for what he had done but for who essentially he was deemed to be.

The result of the unconditional positive regard shown to this man by Jesus is a spontaneous act of reparation expressed in social justice and in the man's personal relationships:

Look, half of my possessions, Lord, I will give to the poor; and if I have
defrauded anyone of anything, I will pay back four times as much. [19,8b]

This indicates, amongst other things, that, to paraphrase Bonhoeffer,
Grace is free but not cheap (Bonhoeffer, 1964, p. 35f) Although a matter
of some conjecture, it could be said that Zacchaeus may have been
saved from sin (or from his sinful self), by his experience of grace in
the one who regarded him so unconditionally and positively. There
is no way of knowing. However, we do know what the story tells
us, that his salvation – his realignment to an authentic life of social
and interpersonal relationships, which at the same time aligned him
with the ground of his being, with Being itself – was engendered by
one who saw and accepted the good in him.

The biblical/theological model of salvation I am arguing for finds
a complementarity beside the emphasis in most forms of counselling
or psychotherapy on helping the client to value themselves. The
similarity here is not merely an interesting likeness but a massive
correspondence with an enormous impact on our understanding
of the human predicament and the solution to that predicament.
Unfortunately, the complementarity here has, ironically, to be
rescued, or at the least elucidated; if it were not, we might conclude
that religion and psychotherapy totally clash at this all-important
place, rather than correspond. In religious terms, the "human
predicament" is popularly portrayed as the sinful nature of "man";
the creature's deviation from and rejection of the will and ways of
the Creator. This condition of sinfulness is commonly understood
as an inflation of the self, referred to more loosely as "selfishness",
which manifests itself in pride, arrogance and the consequent
disregard, neglect and abuse of one's fellow human beings. The
necessary antithesis of and antidote for this condition of "sin", is
to "leave self behind" by turning towards the one true, selfless God
and inseparable from this, towards the needs of others.

This process of moving from sinfulness, selfishness and lost-ness,
to salvation, is not only a popular portrayal but a strong orthodox
emphasis in the faith-tradition of Christianity. In somewhat loose
terms it can be seen as the theological legacy of Augustine of Hippo
(354–430) to Christendom. In its popular form it is never more
evocative than in some of the great evangelical hymns of its worship,
written in the 18th and 19th centuries. The reformed slave-trader,
John Newton (1725–1807), tells of "Amazing grace" responsible for

a miraculous personal transformation: *"I once was lost but now I'm found, was blind but now I see"* (*Hymns and Psalms*, 1983, n. 215, verse 1). Or the less known but equally evocative hymn *In loving-kindness Jesus came* (*The Methodist Hymn Book*, 1933, n. 336) with its rousing heartfelt chorus, *From sinking sands he lifted me; with outstretched arms he lifted me* (n. 336). Perhaps less known but a good sample of the antidote pushed to its limits, is the beautiful, self-effacing hymn of the French writer Theodore Monod (1836–1921) *O The bitter shame and sorrow* (*Hymns and Psalms*, 1983, n. 538), which carries us through a self-discarding spiritual journey which is almost shockingly only fulfilled in self-negation, *None of self, and all of Thee!* (*Hymns and Psalms*, 1983, n. 538, verse 4).

I wish to emphasise that the picture of the (Christian) religious portrayal of sin and salvation outlined above is not without truth. It would be difficult for anyone to deny that as human beings we are capable of gross selfishness and to say that this is a "predicament" would be an understatement. The issue of sin and salvation is more subtle and therefore potentially more confusing and misleading. It revolves, not for the first time in the discussion of this book, around interpretation; more precisely around what in religious and spiritual terms we mean by concepts like "self", "sin", "grace", and most crucially, salvation. I shall not attempt to analyse each of these terms individually but rather to indicate a different model of salvation which is powerfully present in the Bible and the Christian tradition and one which finds a striking complementarity with psychodynamic therapy. It is this latter point which is central to the theme of my exploration: this complementarity strengthens the case for the authenticity of the different model and yet we can readily ignore it, or not be aware of it . Of course, complementarity, as I have sought to demonstrate, is much more than making simple comparisons. It is, amongst other things, an interdisciplinary quest and an aspect of which is both the varied world of counselling models and the world of comparative religion. I mention this now because the salvation model that I have called "popular" as well as "orthodox" is not characteristic of all faith traditions. Judaism, for example, does not see the "human predicament" and its resolution in God in the same way as Christianity. In particular there is not the same emphasis or preoccupation with sin. Certainly there is within Jewish faith a full acknowledgement of human frailty, failure and weakness and the inevitable consequences of this in getting things wrong, sometimes badly wrong, but sin is not the focus or the most important factor of our human condition. (I am indebted to Stephen Dawes [see bibliography] for pointing this out and for a most helpful subsequent conversation and email correspondence (October 2006).

When we bear in mind that the historical Jesus was a person of Jewish faith and not a "Christian", then challenging the "popular" (even if orthodox) view of salvation and sin within Christianity becomes not only an interesting exercise but a necessary one.

If Christian religion speaks of resolution for the human predicament in terms of salvation, the corresponding process within psychotherapy is what one writer refers to as "psychotherapeutics" (J. Klein, 1995, esp. ch.3); that is to say, how people get better, or how we become more whole. Psychotherapeutics refers to the process clients/patients experience in the therapy sessions and beyond, which allows them to move meaningfully and purposefully towards authenticity, integrity, healing or individuation. Of course this barrage of teasing words can become a smoke-screen, or an intellectualization, avoiding the begging question of exactly how we decide what characterises "authenticity", "individuation" and the rest. Making judgements for oneself and developing a philosophy of life is not a pious pursuit, or even a prerogative of the religious; it is an inescapable process for all of us. The therapist who works psychodynamically does not, as a rule of thumb, disclose her or his personal belief system. The reason for this self-imposed boundary is not, I find, easily understood; not even by some who are training to be or practising as counsellors. It is, however, crucial when working psychodynamically that this boundary is taken seriously, since it relates to how people get better. Unless the counsellor regards this self-disclosure boundary seriously, transference and countertransference are likely to be missed or avoided. The importance of these missed opportunities is that counsellor and client are not able to grapple or seriously "play" with, the issues offered in the transference.

Another reason for the counsellor's "rule of abstinence" as it is sometimes called, related to the transference, is that if the counsellor freely shares her or his beliefs, or opinions, this may distract from the need of the client to make their own judgements. The delicate art of allowing the other to move forward by growing in self-esteem, which entails having confidence in the human right to make personal choices, requires the therapist to "stand back" and allow the experience of self-discovery for the other. None of this, however, prevents or excuses the therapist from having convictions, or we might say, a philosophy of life.

It may appear to some that Christian religion and therapy are, at least in this vital area of salvation verses psychotherapeutics, not merely markedly different but diametrically opposed. After all, Christian religion requires believers to promote faith, either by "evangelising" or "witnessing". The difference between these two expressions of the Christian life is critical (I have already expressed my scepticism regarding "evangelism") but they are both, in the common use of these two words, explicit ways of commending faith to others. In the first, we are told about God and/or Jesus, in order for sinners to be saved. In the second, although less explicit, a demonstration of the life of faith is required. We might say that a salient point of Christian religion and of the personal faith of a believer, is to give credit where it is due, or to put it in more traditional and religious terms, to "give glory to God" On the other hand, the therapist seeks to preserve a strong degree of anonymity, providing the other with a relationship context in which they have opportunity to express and struggle with their own issues of self-doubt and fear but, it is hoped, work through this to enjoy the liberating experience of self-determination.

The difference between Christian religion and therapy, related to salvation and psychotherapeutics, is real but it is not a fundamental contradiction. It is rather, part of the difference of complementarity, and complementarity can cope with difference because that is its nature. To flourish, a person requires nurturing, teaching and guiding; good advice and good examples on which to base his or her life, and the love and affirmation of others. However, these external influences, introjected by everyone who has opportunity to do so from the moment of conception, belong to a paradoxical whole, which also requires that a person finds a sense of their intrinsic value *from within*. Without this self-esteem, no amount of affirming, let alone telling, will convince a person that they are "alright"; and yet to live a life without receiving any affirmation of one's self would be utterly desolate

The therapeutic process focuses on the individual's sense of self-worth, by facilitating, or evoking, self-determination and allowing a movement from dependence to independence. I have acknowledged that this presupposes that the therapist holds a conviction – even though this may not be disclosed explicitly to the client – that it is both possible and desirable (healthy) to realize such a sense of self-worth. I have never met and would not expect to meet, a therapist who does not hold such a view, whether openly acknowledged or not. An essential role of religion – perhaps when all is said and done *the* essential role – is to carry, cherish, celebrate and proclaim, in word and deed, the explicit message that within the centre of all life and therefore every individual life, there is a personal God, who is not merely loving but love itself and that this love is by definition understanding, forgiving and accepting; its burden is light and it requires nothing more, yet nothing less than to "accept the fact that you are accepted!" (Tillich, 1949, p. 163).

Faith claims, and proclaims, that there is a need for each of us to hear – even if we cannot or need not hear it through religion – that life has "grace" at its heart; that we can trust ourselves to life and that it will not ultimately disappoint and destroy us but rather enfold and uphold us.

Some of the statements made above are of course ones of faith; they are included here as part of my ongoing attempt to describe the essential nature of religious belief. They also arise out of the experience of working with and within the complementarity being explored. Some of the convictions expressed therefore are matters of theological and religious belief; others can be made and believed in, without adherence to religion. Working with complementarity does not produce tidy answers but – to pick up a previous analogy – invites us to sail on the open sea, into which many rivers, streams and tributaries flow.

Religion and therapy serve differing purposes within a holistic process of healing. They function in considerably different contexts and hold different briefs, but their underlying dynamics, in terms of self-worth, relationships and responsibility are similar, often remarkably similar. That this may not appear to be the case is largely due to ignorance, misunderstanding and misinterpretation. It is important to acknowledge however that both in the case of religion and therapy there can be misrepresentation and bad modelling. In the case of therapy or counselling, the emphasis on self-actualization is sometimes seen as self-indulgence, or "navel-gazing". If, sadly, that is sometimes the case it should be identified as a distortion of the purpose of therapy. There are, of course, dangers that the pursuit of self-actualization may promote an unhealthy focus on oneself but deviations do not negate the true purpose of self-actualization, which when carefully understood is concerned with relationship, within oneself and between oneself, others, and creation. The aim of counselling is not self-indulgence but taking responsibility for oneself.

Religion may also be dismissed through ignorance, misunderstanding and misinterpretation. Religion, like therapy, can also be guilty of misrepresentation and worse, hypocrisy. Such misrepresentation and hypocrisy has caused immeasurable damage to the Church and to those beyond who have been misled, or had their trust in the Church betrayed, yet none of this, however deplorable and regrettable, negates the value of the faith which has integrity.

It does seem that one of the central problems we struggle with as human beings is the breathtaking degree of power we potentially have, even though many are denied this because of political and social control or oppression. As individuals this power frequently proves too much to handle and we either abuse it, by threatening and bullying others in an attempt to escape our insecure feelings, or relinquish it by assuming an inferior, dependent, relationship to others. The latter scenario is all too prevalent within religion and extends to our relationship with God; the dependency, or subservience, allows the believer to be "justified" by putting faith in one who has achieved obedience to God on their behalf. As the ever popular Passiontide hymn says:

There was no other good enough
To pay the price of sin;
He only could unlock the gate
Of heaven, and let us in. [Hymns and Psalms, 1983, n. 178, verse 4]

Such sentiments effectively rob us of even entertaining the idea that we may enjoy even a small measure of inherent goodness or worthiness. This negation of any goodness which we might genuinely and modestly say is ours, is effectively repressed in some religious people, who cannot pass an exam, or perhaps even cross the road safely, without attributing it to divine intervention. What is repressed, of course, comes out elsewhere, in distorted and damaging ways.

The dilemma outlined above is another example of the failing to live with paradox, or to put it another way: we split the paradox (and thereby destroy it as a paradox) by either using our power for selfish ends, or by fleeing from it. Religion is all too often used to flee power, by attributing power to others and to God.

It might be helpful to think of all this in terms of a thesis, antithesis and synthesis. Although in psychotherapy the growth of independence from dependency is often taken as a model, or an indication, of the process towards healthiness, a more accurate indicator would be a movement towards a certain kind of interdependence. I hope the reader will see that even the word "interdependence" is indicative of paradox; it provides the synthesis in the struggle between dependence and independence.

Many years ago, when I was a member of an interviewing panel, a colleague asked the interviewee (a prospective candidate for the ordained ministry of the Church) "Have you the confidence to be humble?" My immediate feeling was one of relief that I wasn't the candidate, whose fumbled reply reflected exactly how I felt! The phrase never left me and given the advantages of time and experience, I began to grasp its wisdom and (inevitably) its profound, paradoxical nature. Of course, as I have previously mentioned, a person of religious faith will consciously or unconsciously acknowledge ultimate dependency on God; beings are not Being-itself. But the dynamic, interpersonal theology I have commended allows us to embrace, even if with some fear and trembling, our own intrinsic goodness as those created in the image of God; those, who are enthused (literally, *have God within*) with the divine presence; daughters and sons of God; God's self-expression.

The above picture of a saving religion, which falls into the trap of using the saving motif to effectively rob the believer of self-esteem and self-determination, is a collusive process. That is to say, the believer unconsciously but readily accepts the formula of total unworthiness. It may also be part of the price paid for rejecting dualism. It is as though in rejecting a separate source of evil, we find ourselves bereft of somewhere to locate it, at which point we are perhaps unconsciously but acutely aware that we might have to take responsibility for evil ourselves, or put more positively, the responsibility of being essentially good. This responsibility is frequently too much for us to bear and the resolution is sought by misuse of a saviour figure, guaranteed to be successful because the figure is divine. "God", (when seen as a thoroughly theistic being) comes to our rescue in Christ and by his "atonement", our sins are taken away. However, (so the theory goes) because a righteous God cannot simply overlook unrighteousness, a price has to be paid – the horrendous death of God's only begotten Son – who through his sacrifice pays this ransom on our behalf and thereby sets us free from the inevitable deadly consequences. Although this is a common view of the "atonement" within Christian religion, I do not endorse it. There is, however, a flip side to this; a mirror image. All too often an excessive sense of sinfulness and unworthiness is the necessary requirement for being the recipient of a rescue operation – a saving from sin. The cycle of self-disgust, despair, confession, in which one "throws" oneself on the mercy of God, and God's saving act in Jesus Christ, effectively makes sure that God takes responsibility and not me!

I have often struggled to understand the psychological process that is operative in a saving religion which requires and promotes the necessity for its adherents to regard themselves as worthless and to confess this before God, before receiving forgiveness and acceptance. As is often the case when one struggles in such a way, the light dawned, or the penny dropped, in a moment of "givenness". It was not a question of trawling through psychological theories in a vain attempt to fish out an answer but a sudden realization that psychodynamic therapy, provides a particular concept which converges strikingly and undeniably at this point, with this religious phenomenon.

What then is this psychological aspect of a convergence which leads to a powerful area of complementarity? It is that particular and complex form of projection called *projective identification*. The reader may remember that in my earlier references to projective identification I said: "Projective identification, it should be noted, involves not only the so called bad parts of the self; that which is split off and projected can be "good"." In the case of unhealthy projection, feelings of self-worth are rejected and in the counselling situation can be projectively identified within the (idealized) counsellor. When this dumping process occurs in therapy it will almost certainly have antecedents in the client's life history and especially her or his childhood; the roots are invariably an idealized parent. The client has not experienced a natural and healthy disillusionment of parents, most likely because of a considerable (unconscious) fear of having to accept a less than good enough view of the parent. As a child, this realistic view, even when defended against by idealization, impacts negatively upon the child, for it does not take long for a child who experiences abusive or neglectful parenting, to feel that the way in which he or she has been treated equates to who and how the child considers herself or himself to be. This is what I call a "double whammy", which the dictionary defines as "*a devastating setback made up of two elements*" (*Collins Concise Dictionary*, 1982).

It needs to be stressed that the projection, in the particular form of projective identification, which I am referring to, is unconscious and that the word "idealized" is of utmost importance, for the client unconsciously resents giving up his own good and having it at arms length in the counsellor (or another). Klein makes clear elsewhere that projectively identifying good things in the other serves a positive, healthy purpose in the baby's relationship to mother. This however, is during what Klein calls the *paranoid schizoid position* when a large measure of splitting is inevitable. It is akin to the pre-disillusionment state I refer to above. In a later, more mature state this would be unhealthy.

The client's projective identification of their good "parts" gives us considerable insight into the religious scenario of the perceived need of the "sinner" to placate himself/herself before a righteous God who requires an acknowledgement of utter worthlessness before acceptance. Sadly, such a "spiritual" process invariably fosters a sense of the sinner's lack of self-worth, since anything of goodness which the sinner might enjoy and take pride in, is deposited with God, where it can be kept safe; that is, where the sinner is not in danger of having to live joyfully and adventurously, by taking responsibility and exercising their own goodness

Perhaps it is easier and less frightening for all of us, on occasions, to deny our goodness and powerfulness, by allowing someone else to carry it. The unconscious element of this is a lack of self-esteem and a feeling of inferiority, which keeps us tied to our sense of unworthiness and causes us to relinquish personal responsibility. Religion can all too often aid and abet this unhealthy process by an over-emphasis on our "sinful" nature and at the same time by discouraging or condemning self-expression and personal pride, which is assumed to be self indulgence and arrogance, rather than creativity and the experience of taking a natural delight in the gift of one's self and of others.

Nelson Mandela is, I think, saying something similar in quoting these startling words:

Our deepest fear is not that we are inadequate.
Our deepest fear is that we are powerful beyond measure.
It is our light, not our darkness, that most frightens us.
We ask ourselves: "Who am I to be brilliant, gorgeous, talented, fabulous?"
Actually, who are we not to be?
You are a child of God. Your playing small doesn't serve the world.
There's nothing enlightened about shrinking so that other people around you won't feel insecure.
We are all meant to shine, as children do.
We are born to manifest the glory of God that is within us.
It is not just in some of us; it is in everyone.
And as we let our light shine, we unconsciously give other people permission to do the same.
As we are liberated from our own fear, our presence automatically liberates others.

Although frequently attributed to Mandela, the source of these words is Marianne Williamson (Williamson, 1992, Section 3 of Chapter 7).

It is enormously important to recognise that the vast majority of people who seek help in counselling, for one reason or another, suffer not from thinking of themselves too highly but from a lack of self-esteem. It is not unusual, in my experience, to hear a client/ patient say, "I loath myself", or a variation of that theme.

Of course it may be said and has been, particularly from a critical psychological perspective by Freud, that the concept of God in traditional theism is (like the Devil) also an externalising, objectifying and distancing of the fears and anxieties of humankind. The rejection of Freud's ideas, especially his views on religion, can easily become a knee-jerk reaction by the religiously committed. In psychological terms this might be understood as a defence against facing unpalatable truths which reside within ourselves. An important insight of psychodynamic thinking is that we know many things of which we are not aware, sometimes because we choose to repress the unpalatable.

I shall return to Freud's view of religion and particularly of God as a human projection, in the next chapter, where there is a convergence between religion and psychology which points to a particularly challenging complementarity for the person of faith. For the moment it can be seen from the brief indication given of my own theology that I would not wish to dismiss Freud's ideas entirely. His rejection of God as an external being (or any other kind of being) is not entirely inconsistent with the view of Macquarrie who is not content to see God described as a being, even if the biggest and best of beings. If that element of theism which seeks to emphasise and preserve the sovereignty and independence of God is taken too literally it diminishes and demeans the mystery and "otherness" of the One who cannot be finally contained or named; such a limited view of God deserves to be rejected.

If a more dynamic, ambivalent and less categorical concept of God were allowed, some of those who reject traditional Christianity might find it more believable. The psychoanalyst, Charles Rycroft, would seem to fall into this category. In an essay entitled Causes and Meaning, he writes:

> Recent developments in theology…make it very doubtful whether cosmology can be regarded as the central religious idea or whether belief in a God "out there" is the essence of the religious attitude. Although we can have no idea of what Freud personally would have made of Bonhoeffer's "religionless Christianity", or of Zen Buddhism, or of statements like Guntrip's: "the fundamental therapeutic factor in psychotherapy is more akin to religion than to science, since it is a matter of personal relationship…religion has always stood for the good object relationship", there would seem to be no necessary incompatibility between psychoanalysis and those religious formulations which locate God within the self. One could, indeed, argue that Freud's id (and even more Groddeck's "it"), the impersonal force within which is both the core of oneself and yet not oneself, and from which in illness one becomes alienated, is a secular formulation of the insight which makes religious people believe in an immanent God: if this were so, psychoanalysis could be regarded as a semantic bridge between science and biology on the one hand and religion and the humanities on the other. [Rycroft, 1966, p. 50f]

I am not commending Rycroft's view as an adequate formulation of Christian theology, neither of course is Rycroft. Interestingly, in as much as he is venturing into theology, Rycroft falls short in a similar way to Robinson in the 1960s, by simply substituting the location of God from "out there" to "within the self". However, it seemed at the time that Robinson was moving in the right direction and despite Macquarrie's outright rejection of Tillich's phraseology, implicit in Robinson's impressionable *Honest to God*, it did seem to be a crucial step along the way to a more realistic and imaginative way and not least a more personal way of conceptualizing the divine. In retrospect it was a necessary and welcome antithesis to an over-emphasis on a metaphysical, transcendent model of deity. It also opened the way for attempts to find, not so much a synthesis as a departure from a static view which, even in Tillich, suffers from too much association with the concept of location.

James Mann's foundational work on time-limited psychotherapy (Mann, 1973), is an intensive and sophisticated development of psychodynamic therapy in which time is used throughout as a powerful therapeutic tool and which therefore may be more helpfully described as time-conscious, time-sensitive, or time-focused therapy. This form of treatment gives a working model with which to assess the focus of a person's pathology. Arising from a *Substantive Base* of maturation, as growth from anxiety separation to individuation, he posits four *Basic Universal Conflict Situations*: Independence versus dependence, Activity versus passivity, Adequate self-esteem versus diminished or loss of self-esteem and Unresolved or delayed grief. (The latter of these categories is better balanced with the addition of a phrase such as, "versus resolved grief or adequate mourning") Mann does not expect the therapist to recognise one of these conflict situations to be exclusively relevant and freely admits that all four have a part to play. In practice therefore the therapist finds that one of the four is closely linked to another. This is inevitable when all four arise from the same Substantive Base. In my experience the prominent conflict situation is time and again adequate self-esteem versus diminished or loss of self-esteem, often followed closely by and intrinsically linked to one or more of the remaining three conflict situations.

It is ironic that religion often gives the impression that one of our most hideous "sins" is our tendency to regard ourselves too highly; so much so that, invariably, a prerequisite for approaching the presence of God is to recognise and acknowledge not only our utter unworthiness but our deplorable state. I have already referred in this chapter to the Augustinian influence in the shaping of a sin-focused theology. To this we must add the later but not dissimilar influence of John Calvin and the Calvinistic tradition, in which human nature (after the Biblical "fall") is regarded as essentially sinful. Even some of the finest hymns of the 18th century written by Charles Wesley betray this characteristic; for example, Wesley's hymn of praise, in which the "sinner" sings lustily *"Vilest of the sinful race, Lo! I answer to Thy call..."* (*The Methodist Hymn Book*, 1933, n. 574, verse 2), and in verse 3, *"If so poor a worm as I may to Thy great glory live..."* The compilers of the current hymn book, officially used in the Methodist Church, implicitly acknowledge that the above phrases are unacceptable, omitting the second verse altogether and by changing verse 3 to *"If a sinner such as I..."* (*Hymns and Psalms*, 1983, n. 791). The former wording, was consistently used until the publication of *Hymns and Psalms* in 1983 and still is in churches which continue to use the "old" book. The unrevised wording implies the necessity for worshippers to plead for forgiveness, which in turn is a prerequisite for hearing and receiving God's forgiveness. Careful reflection on the story about Jesus offers a quite different understanding of what Jesus' religion is about, as I have tried to demonstrate in the touchstone example of Zacchaeus. If that understanding were to be reflected in the Church's liturgy – and by "liturgy" I imply not only prescribed written forms of Service but the whole tenor of worship, communicated through choice of hymns, songs, sermons and prayers – there would be a much greater emphasis on the accepting, forgiving presence of God. Opportunities to respond would naturally follow, rather than the too readily assumed sequence of repentance *followed by* a declaration of God's forgiveness. It is true that since the ecumenically based work of the Liturgical Movement in the 1960s and the renewed Orders of Service which that movement generated, we have seen a vast improvement. Nevertheless, it seems that the pull towards a "we repent, God forgives us" mind set is not an easy one to leave behind. It is unusual and refreshing therefore to discover theologians who state in a clear, understandable way, the essence of the gospel message of Jesus, or we might say more pointedly, of Jesus who is God's Good News. Leander Keck is such a theologian:

> ...if you had to state the central theme of Jesus' teaching, what would it be?....according to Matthew 4.17 the theme of Jesus' teaching is, "Repent, for the kingdom of heaven is at hand." Luke gives us three things

to be understood: repentance, the kingdom of heaven and the relation between them. In Matthew the kingdom of heaven does not refer to the place where people go after death – to heaven; rather, the kingdom of heaven means exactly the same as the kingdom of God. This is because in such phrases heaven is a way of referring to God without actually using the word. It's also important that we understand repentance, as Jesus and Matthew use it. It represented a Hebrew word, T'shuvah, which means "turning around". Jesus used "repentance" the way Old Testament prophets used it. He called to turn away from one way of life and towards another. "Repentance" is neither feeling sorry for having sinned, nor penance – making up for it. Repentance is turning life God-ward. What then is the relation between God's kingdom and repentance? According to Jesus' preaching we are to repent because the kingdom is at hand. Now according to Matthew, John the Baptist had said exactly the same thing; yet what a difference between them. How do we account for that? Quite simply, for John the Baptist, people were to repent in order to be ready for the kingdom. But according to Jesus we repent in response to the kingdom. Everything depends on understanding the difference. According to Matthew, the Sermon on the Mount does not give us the requirement that must be met before the kingdom can come but the kind of response we are able to make because God's kingdom has come near to us in Jesus. Unfortunately, most churches' preaching is closer to John the Baptist than to Jesus. [Keck, 1996]

CHAPTER NINE

The presence of God and the capacity to be alone

In the last chapter a significant and perhaps to some, surprising area of complementarity was highlighted; psychotherapeutics and the Christian process of salvation have a great deal in common regarding our lack of self-esteem and our corresponding need for acceptance in which we are treated with positive, unconditional regard. That is not to say that therapy and religion offer the same pathway in seeking to resolve this need but that there is a significant convergence and a strong complementarity in what they have to say about what makes people healthy.

Having made use of one of James Mann's *Universal Conflict Situations* in the last chapter, that of adequate self-esteem versus diminished or loss of self-esteem, I shall now turn to another of Mann's areas of conflict to support the next illustration of complementarity, namely, Independence versus dependence. This conflict situation is already familiar to the reader in the context of these pages and not least in the last chapter. This is not surprising when it is remembered that Mann derives all four of these "situations" from the same *Substantive Base* of the recurring struggle, throughout life, of growth from separation anxiety to individuation. It is virtually impossible to speak of one of these four without exploring the relationship to the others. However, when we are considering areas of complementarity, one of the four will have a leading role and will provide the main concept for interpretation.

I have already emphasised that the biblical picture of the believer's relationship with God is one of utter dependency and that this is axiomatic, not least in terms of my own theological outlook: God is not a separate Being but to use Ford's terminology: "...the condition for the possibility of the existence of anything..." (Ford, 2003, p. 10). In religious language, the point regarding ultimate dependency remains the same. The true believer is one who gives herself/ himself to God completely. In the Christian tradition, without the indwelling of Christ and an acknowledgement of his supremacy, the disciple "can do nothing" (John 15,5). Indeed, Paul of Tarsus, who was so influential in the shaping of the early Christian communities, declares that "... it is no longer I who live, but it is Christ who lives in me..." (Galatians 2,20a).

Although utter dependency on God as one who creates and continually sustains all things is an a priori monotheistic concept, If interpreted unimaginatively and in a non-paradoxical way, it can result in a depreciation of one's self and the relinquishing of personal responsibility. It may also convey the impression, whether intended or not, that "I", as the believer, am quite indifferent to the needs of my neighbour. After all, if Christ "fills" the believer's life, why should the "I" of that believer need to take responsibility? Indeed, students of the Bible are well aware of how this misconception, or more likely, rationalization, is clearly indicated as an on-going problem for the apostle Paul in his relationships with some of the communities of believers who were converted from paganism under his influence. The "antinomians" (literally, "those against the law") were delighted to be told that they were saved not by their good works but by God's grace demonstrated in Christ and responded to with faith. If I may paraphrase in a clumsy way to make the point, "If we are saved by grace", they speculated, "if it is all down to God and there is nothing we can do to improve our standing before God, we may as well go on sinning and enjoy doing so, for does it not follow that in doing so, we not only enjoy sinning but increasingly evoke and receive grace?" The biblical text puts it much more succinctly: "What then are we to say? Should we continue in sin in order that grace may abound? By no means!" (Romans 6,1-2a). Bonhoeffer's theme rings out again: "Grace is free but not cheap!"

The recurring words that the believer should do everything "in the name of Christ" or "for Christ's sake" is another variation on the theme of this doctrine and prone to similar abuse. When misunderstood, its ludicrousness is seen in the corny "joke" in which the lady of the manor agrees to give the tramp at her door a crust of bread. Intent on making her "witness", she prefaces her gift by saying: "I want you to know, my man, that I'm giving you this for Christ's sake." To which the tramp replies, "Then for Christ's sake, lady, put some butter on it."

My reason for labouring the above point is that Christian believers too often assume, at least theoretically, a distorted understanding of the utter dependency model as the basis for relationship with God. Self-development and self-worth are, explicitly or implicitly, regarded as selfishness; a form of false modesty ensues, which, ironically, has a feel of arrogance and empty piety about it. Underlying and driving this model is a simplistic theology, which envisages God as a distanced being who somehow needs to be invited into the believer's life (usually referred to as the "heart"). Conversely, the believer needs to relinquish personal ambition, passion and self-interest, in order to give himself or herself in complete obedience to "the will of God." It might well be that a motivation for such unimaginative understandings of dependency on God is an unconscious wish to avoid personal responsibility. This is effectively an aspect of the point made in the last chapter regarding the sinner's unconscious need to be devoid of any goodness.

The "splitting" which occurs in the believer, who regards himself and all others as a separate entity from "God", is also a form of defence against an acceptance of the ambivalent nature of creation's relationship to its Creator – "Being itself." Putting this in terms of human beings, we might say that the ambivalence reflects the awesome truth of the paradox that on the one hand beings are not identical with Being itself but on the other hand beings are intrinsically related to Being. It is common enough to emphasise the *difference* side of the paradox since difference can easily (and conveniently) be misunderstood as *distance*, at which point of course the paradox is destroyed and splitting has occurred. When the paradox is retained and we opt to live with the ambivalence, we are faced with the challenge of how to manage a relationship with the God who is closer than breathing. Indeed I have gone further in already suggesting that creatures are not only creations of the Creator but the Creator's *self-expression*. I suspect that this is often "too close for comfort". The rejection of such closeness and such ambivalence, may be consciously expressed as a respect for

God's otherness, holiness and sovereignty. The unconscious motive, however, may be an avoidance of holiness, lest its presence is a blessing which disturbs and challenges us; the fear of living with the responsibility of being a "child of God". The latter phrase is much-loved and seemingly uncontroversial but is it very different from saying "a god of God"?

Although the dependency model of relationship with God has, in certain ways, motivated many Christian saints and left a colossal mark for good on humankind, in its more stark and unimaginative forms it carries a strange contradiction. On the one hand, "following Christ" always implies a valuing and empowering of the believer and yet, what I've termed, the dependency model – if misinterpreted, as it so easily can be and frequently is – devalues and disempowers the believer. This discrepancy cannot be explained or justified by describing the dependency model as itself "paradoxical" for it fails to embody what is the nub of a paradox – the holding together in creative tension of two seemingly contradictory elements. To emphasise the point: the dependency model fails because it splits the two elements of the paradox (dependency and independence) and treats them as though they were genuine opposites, which the potential believer has to choose between.

I want to argue, not for a total rejection of the concept of dependency, for it is self-evident, but that it should be understood profoundly and paradoxically rather than simplistically. Issues around the subjects of self, dependency and attachment are plentiful and complex within psychodynamic thinking. What indications of complementarity might there be which could point us in the direction of authentic, wholesome relationships and at the same time offer a meaningful psychological framework for the Christian concept of dependency on God?

In 1957 W.D. Winnicott, the paediatrician and psychoanalyst, delivered a short paper entitled, "The Capacity to be Alone". The brevity of this paper is deceptive for it is a masterpiece of insight and profundity. Winnicott describes the capacity to be alone as: "…one of the most important signs of maturity in emotional development" (Winnicott, 1958, p. 29). This in itself is interesting in the context of our discussion, since a great deal of popularised Christian thinking and behaviour demonstrates our need for others and supremely for God. Superficially, therefore, complementarity in this area seems not only hard to find but quite inappropriate. It is not only religion which demonstrates this problem. In his own field of study Winnicott says: "It is probably true to say that in psycho-analytical literature more has been written on the *fear* of being alone or the *wish* to be alone than on the *ability* to be alone..." (*ibid.*, p 29). However, superficiality is not what we are concerned with and in fact a little attention given to this subject reveals one of the most vital and enlightening areas of complementarity between religion and psychology. Winnicott makes clear that his concept of "being alone" can only be understood paradoxically: "...the basis of the capacity to be alone is a paradox; it is the experience of being alone while someone else is present" (*ibid.*, p 30). The "someone" for Winnicott is originally the mother (or mother-substitute), who is present for her child or at least "represented for the moment by a cot or a pram or the general atmosphere of the immediate environment" (*ibid.*, p 30).

This last quotation is important, because it catches the essence of the paradox (mother present yet not present) and therefore provides an appropriate and powerful picture for understanding the paradoxical nature of a believer's relationship with God. I need to clarify here that Winnicott's concept is of a mature emotional state; the picture he paints, of a child in the presence of mother (or mother-substitute), is the *basic experience* which determines how successfully a capacity to be alone is developed in adult life.

Winnicott illustrates the capacity to be alone in adult life by referring to the experience of a couple immediately after experiencing sexual intercourse, in which "...each partner is alone and is contented to be alone. Being able to enjoy being alone along with another person who is also alone is in itself an experience of health" (*ibid.*, p 31). We may note, in raising this point, that it is a loss to theology that Christian writers have not frequently used the language and experience of human sexuality to gain insight into spiritual experience. This is due, no doubt, to the jaundiced view, which Christianity has often held and fostered regarding sexuality. Thankfully, there are some notable exceptions, especially amongst the Mystics, such as St John of the Cross.

Winnicott develops and supports his theory by referring to the work of Melanie Klein. The reader will remember, or may wish to refer back to, earlier comments on Klein which now find their place within this current discussion. Klein's theory of the cyclical process of introjection and projection in the infant's experience leads, in the healthy person, to the establishment of: "…a good object in the psychic reality of the individual" (ibid., p. 32).

"Good-enough mothering" (perhaps the most popular of Winnicott's concepts) allows the growing child to internalise a good experience of the mother so that when she is no longer actually present, she remains present, since the experience of her has become integrated within the growing child: "In the course of time the individual introjects the ego-supportive mother and in this way becomes able to be alone without frequent reference to the mother or mother symbol" (ibid., p 32).

The ending of counselling therapy, when it is a healthy one, can occur when the client shows sufficient ability to internalise the experience of being with the therapist/counsellor. The convergence and complementarity around these issues of dependency versus independence are, however, wider, more intricate and thereby more impressive, than this one point, however important in itself.

To express the full range and value of this complementarity, I need to draw attention to a further facet of the counselling situation which in itself complements the growing independence and eventual internalization of the counselling process by the client. Many who seek and engage in counselling suffer from low self-esteem and a fragile sense of self. Approaching a counsellor can, in itself, take enormous effort and requires courage. it can take time for trust to be established and this often requires a period of "holding", during which the counsellor would engage in a lot of listening and reflecting back, therefore letting the client know that she or he is being heard in a care-full way. This stage of the therapy may well be accompanied by the client feeling strongly attached to and dependent on the counsellor. It may also produce a measure of idealization by the client of the counsellor. None of the features of this "holding" period contradicts those of the "good enough" ending I have just spoken of; they are frequently necessary for the good enough ending to take place. In between those "ends", where the therapeutic process continues, the idealizations gives way to an acceptance of loss, perhaps to depression, anger, sadness and to realism and hope. In Kleinian terms, the client is helped to spend less time in the "schizoid-paranoid position" and more in the "depressive position".

Once again, looking at this intricacy goes right to the heart of the complementarity methodology used throughout this book, for we are not strictly speaking about using psychology to interpret religion, or vice versa but standing back and allowing two distinctly different disciplines and experiences to shine their light on essentially the same constellation of truths.

By implication, I am suggesting that Winnicott's concept of The Capacity to be Alone, and the comments I have made immediately above, find their counterpart in the believer's relationship with God. This latter phrase need not be confined to Christian faith, or even a precise religion; the complementarity I am proposing applies to a wide variety of human experiences. The key theme linking each will be the experiences described above. Within Christian faith the story of the Ascension, which we will now briefly consider, is a paradigm of this theme.

The so called "Great Commission" of Matthew's Gospel closes (as does the whole gospel) with the words "And remember, I am with you always, even to the end of the age" (Matthew 28,20b). These words are attributed to the post-resurrection Jesus who is about to finally separate from his disciples in a physical form but who assures them that he will continue with them. This same experience is portrayed in the closing words of Luke's Gospel when Jesus bestows a blessing on the disciples but in the precise moment of doing so "...he withdrew from them and was carried up into heaven" (Luke 24,51).

The historical basis for the story of the Ascension is not my present concern; nor, I suspect, was it the concern of those who recorded the story. What is important is the mystical nature of a spiritual experience, which is necessarily paradoxical. With Winnicott's Capacity to be Alone in mind, we might say, "mother is not present/ mother is present" is paralleled here by "Jesus is not present/Jesus is present", or to put a finer point on it, "Jesus is not present/Christ is present." Even the writers of the New Testament cannot always contain the paradox in its pure form. John's account has Jesus saying to his disciples "...if I do not go away, the Advocate* will not come to you; but if I go, I will send him to you" (John 16, 7b). Here there is, so to speak, a straight swap: a spiritual (invisible) presence for the (physical) presence of Jesus. In reality however, there seem to be no grounds for making a distinction between the Holy Spirit and the presence of the post-ascension Jesus. The Acts of the Apostles uses a similar split image, in which the disciples are promised the gift of the Holy Spirit in replacement for the physical presence of Jesus. In fact that is not quite true, since living with the "replacement" is a more spiritually mature stage of faith development; the disciples can now do *more* than before Jesus' death. In a counselling or therapeutic context, this latter point is evident in the more mature, or healthier, client who has internalized the therapist (or better I think, the therapeutic process), and concluded the therapy rather than continued with it.

We can now see that far from being contradictory (or merely plain nonsense), the reality of these ascension stories can be understood (as one example) alongside Winnicott's picture of the capacity to be alone. As the growing child introjects his experience of the mother, so the believer introjects an experience of Christ. The Christ element is real but if thoroughly digested, becomes integrated within the believer. This is, of course, a *process* and not a single act in a moment of time. The process continues as, for example, the believer "feeds upon Christ" – especially depicted in the drama of the Lord's Supper or Holy Communion – and in the "sanctification" of the believer's life, engendered by continual commitment to the Way of Christ. The process may therefore be understood as psychologically the same as when the growing child successfully incorporates a good-enough experience of mother (and the wider, facilitating environment) and is able to live independently of her, or, as we have said above, the way in which the therapy client internalises a good-enough experience of the therapist (or the therapeutic process) to be able to continue the process independent of her actual presence. My earlier references to the presence of God being simultaneously immanent and transcendent, also find a psychological counterpart in Winnicott's paradox of the mother who is present and yet not present. It is, I hope, more evident now why the term "interdependence" is more evocative of real, healthy relationships, rather than "independence" or "dependence".

There is a crucial point which arises from Winnicott's profoundly simple thesis. His comment that there is a scarcity of psychoanalytical literature on the subject of "the *ability* to be alone" (relative to "the *fear* of being alone or the *wish* to be alone"), suggests that the paradoxical nature of the capacity to be alone is resisted within psychotherapeutic circles as it often is within religion. What is this about? It would suggest a trait, not only within religion but in human nature. One of the steepest "learning curves" for the therapist is relinquishing delusions of omnipotence. Most, if not all, beginning therapists/ counsellors enjoy the feeling of power which their position vis `a vis the "patient" can engender. If the trainee is to mature and become an effective practitioner, this feeling of omnipotence has to be acknowledged, faced and let go of. The corollary is a recognition that the client has within herself or himself the capacity to change; the most the therapist can do – and it is no small thing – is to facilitate and encourage that capacity. Neville Symington in his book on narcissism makes this point in a particularly striking way. In referring to emotional corrective experience, he challenges the view, common enough within psychotherapy literature and amongst counsellors, that the therapist provides such a positive experience for the client; the therapist becomes, so to speak, a role model for the client:

> In my view it is the inner action of the patient that corrects the experience. The therapist's job is to understand and illuminate the currents of the inner world, and it is in the light of this experience that the patient corrects the experience through inner mental activity. Freud said that the analyst analyses but the synthetic function, the function where parts become integrated, is provided by the patient. [Symington, 1993, p. 109f]

Symington makes a valid point and one that needs to be heard but perhaps in supplying an antithesis to the view that the patient is reliant on the good example of the therapist for healing to take place, a valuable synthesis is in danger of being lost. The healing which can take place within therapy is about a relationship. On the one hand, a healing process cannot take place unless the client allows self-healing to occur but this individuation takes place, inextricably, not only *within* a relationship but often *because of* the relationship – one in which the therapist shows positive, unconditional regard and thereby provides a "holding" environment and a "modelling" for the client. This reinforces a point made earlier when referring to Person-Centred counselling.

With the above in mind I am driven to ask again why it is commonplace for religious people to keep God at arms length. Conversely, why might it be difficult to accept that God is constantly present within creation and therefore within each human being – not merely as a visiting guest – but as the indispensable "condition for the possibility of the existence of anything and the understanding and practice of anything" (Ford, 2003, p. 10). God is woven into the very fabric of our being. This theme appears to be at the centre of the faith and proclamation of Jesus. His central message that "the kingdom of God has come near; repent, and believe in the good news" (Mark 1.15), is a startling and challenging proclamation that God is not at arms length but to continue the metaphor, "at hand" (*engidso*), which is an alternative translation of "near" in Mark 1,15. Why would this be frightening? In answer to this, I emphasise what has been said in the last chapter: to create a God who is at a safe distance fosters the need for a dependent relationship with God and simultaneously (and again unconsciously) avoids real life-giving engagement with the one whose expression of love we are.

The "capacity to be alone" might be translated in religious terms as the recognition that the other, as well as one's self, is intrinsically good, or is God-imbued and therefore has the inbuilt capacity for what the psychotherapist might call individuation – creative growth. Experiences of what believers term the "Holy Spirit", a subject we will consider in the next and last chapter, may then be understood not as miraculous interventions or intrusions into human life but the religious dimension of that self-healing which finds its secular but perhaps equally spiritual counterpart in the therapeutic experience.

CHAPTER TEN

The Holy Spirit and introjection

The task of Christian apologetics is to make faith more intelligible and therefore less prone to the accusation that it is obscure, magical or bizarre. It cannot – nor should it attempt to – make faith more palatable but it can reduce the possibility of misunderstanding.

One area of Christian theology which is frequently called into question by opponents of religion as well as some affiliated to religion is that which centres around the "Third person of the Trinity" – The "Holy Spirit", (which hereafter, I will refer to as the Spirit, with certain exceptions where the longer title is required.) The fact that the "work" of the Spirit and an experience of the Spirit are considered vital to Christian faith makes it all the more important that the doctrine is presented in as understandable and accessible a way as possible. This is not (in the psychoanalytical sense) reductionism, or (in the theological sense) a form of liberal rationalising. Indeed, it may legitimately be regarded (using Jungian terminology) as an amplification, since as I will argue, like all previous areas I have focused on, it lends itself to an interdisciplinary approach. Once again we thankfully recognize that the social sciences together with the thought-forms of the 21st century have an important role in illuminating and making contemporary, an ancient faith.

The possibility of Christian talk about the Spirit being misunderstood, (or more likely, ridiculed and rejected), is heightened by fundamentalist accounts of the work of the Spirit in a believer's life. An extreme example of this fundamentalist approach is the so-called "Toronto Blessing" This movement began in the mid 1990s and appears to have its origins in the preaching of South African Pentecostalist preacher, Rodney Howard Browne, who moved to America and became an itinerant preacher. To cut a longer story short, Browne's influence spread to others, notably the Toronto Airport Vineyard Church, then under the leadership of John Arnott. Arnott invited a fellow Vineyard pastor in Missouri to preach at the Toronto church. The effects of Clark's preaching included "holy laughter" and a phenomenon referred to as being "slain in the Spirit" and of "drunkenness in the Holy Spirit" often accompanied by leaping, dancing and screaming.

The Toronto Blessing is not particularly noteworthy in itself, except that it produced behaviour which, even compared to many other examples of the outbreak of religious revival, was extreme and widely criticised by many evangelical groups. I mention it because it will still be within living memory of those who read this book. Nor need we doubt the reality of this kind of spiritual phenomenon, which is well documented in the history of religious revival and frequently accompanied by "ecstatic utterance" or "speaking in tongues". This is not to say, of course, that such a phenomenon is free from psychological disturbance; it may indeed be a form of religious neurosis. My purpose in citing revivalist religion is that whilst it is extreme and therefore not representative of religion as a whole, it colours the overall picture of what is presented as the nature, place and purpose of the Spirit. Although accounts of revivalist religion are the extreme end of a spectrum of Spirit-related language and experience, the impression can be given, or received, that most or all Spirit experiences are irrational, intrusive, noisy and lacking any relationship with experiences of ordinary people living ordinary lives.

The above danger of a distorted picture of Spirit talk and experience is exacerbated by the less extreme but nevertheless, simplistic and emotionalized ways in which this doctrine is typically presented in what might be termed packaged religion, characterised by its conscious or unconscious suppression of a non-prescriptive, exploratory faith. The popularity and proliferation of "Alpha" courses is a current example of this religious package approach. This movement which has been pioneered by an Anglican clergyman and is based at Holy Trinity Church, Brompton, offers a combination of video presentations, discussion groups and the sharing of a simple meal. Alpha enjoyed phenomenal growth throughout the 1990s. Its gatherings are often interlaced with contemporary Christian songs. There are some good, well-tried and tested ingredients in these meetings: friendship, food and music, for example. No doubt these factors have provided a welcoming and enjoyable experience for many. The course itself offers Christian teaching particularly designed to help people who are not committed to Christian faith but wish to know more. My own experience of attending a Course and my impression of other such courses, is that its support is largely drawn from those who are either within or around the life of the organised Church.

The logo of Alpha is beguiling and potentially misleading. The large-writ question mark indicates an encouragement for the seeker to enquire. Whilst this may well be the case (it was not in practice mine), it needs to be noted that answers to any questions are not only available but are irrefutable. Furthermore, they are supplied from the Bible, via the doctrinal formulations of Alpha Course theology. In the last resort this packaged religion approach is doctrinaire, exclusive and leaves no room for the development of a mature faith in which openness of mind, creative reinterpretation and positive doubt are crucial.

Pruyser is profoundly perceptive in his reflections on and critique of religious fundamentalism and aspects of evangelicalism. His writings are of particular interest and of rare quality because, whilst writing from a perspective of personal faith, he offers insightful psychological descriptions of healthy, "mature" religion and that which is "neurotic".

Pruyser pulls no punches in his criticism of what he sees as a "Sacrifice of the Intellect":

"...Numbers of professing Christians see manifestations of the Holy Spirit in such unreasonable acts as babbling and having fits, as if the Third Person had no intelligence, no shrewdness, no reason." [Pruyser, 1977b, p. 50]

Pruyser concludes: "Sacrifice of the intellect, demanded by a good many religious movements and blithely if not joyously made by a good many religious persons, is surely one of the ominous features of neurotic religion" (Pruyser, 1977c, p. 51).

Leaving aside both the lunatic fringe and the growing tide of less extreme but simplistic evangelicalism, we are left with a firm, well-attested tradition of faith-experience in which believers speak of spiritual indwelling and transformation. These experiences are a continuation of a central biblical theme in both the Jewish and Christian scriptures. I am thinking particularly of those stories in which individuals receive or take in the Spirit, resulting, for example, in the declaration of the apostle Paul referred to in the previous chapter: "...it is no longer I who live, but it is Christ who lives in me...." (Galatians 2,20a).

I have already made fleeting reference in the previous chapter to the most graphic and symbolic example of this in-taking: the command of the historical Jesus to eat bread (and drink wine) as an act of remembrance. These "words of institution" are intended not merely as an aide memoir but as a "means of grace" whereby the believer symbolically ingests the person of Christ; in reality, by identification and discipleship, until gradually and as a dynamic process, the person is spiritually nourished and fortified. In the mature stages of this spiritual process it is impossible and irrelevant to clearly distinguish between the believer and the indwelling Christ; a physical counterpart would be to say that we become what we eat.

To understand this ingestion in personal terms only would be a betrayal of its holistic implications and the holistic nature of the Christian message. It would make the mistake of not only over-personalizing it but privatising it; a mistake (or perhaps more accurately an escapism) all too common amongst the religious. Just as the real cross with its paradoxical message of obscene cruelty and irrepressible love can be rendered powerless when encased in a stained glass window, so this simplest of profound actions can become a lifeless ritual rather than an inspirational drama that calls us again and again to faith in the real world.

If the "words of institution" are responded to in a reader-responsive criticism mode, we might correct the imbalance referred to above by recognising its social and political dimensions. Thankfully we need never have heard about reader-responsive criticism to do so; an imaginative and rooted faith might intuitively achieve this. The presence of the "Real Christ" can be seen therefore, not only as a personal faith experience but as a command to *re-member* (or "put back together") the crushed, or dis-membered "body" of Christ (symbolised in the broken bread and poured out wine). To put it in another way, followers of the Christ are to be living examples of re-formulating the whole of society where its brokenness, represented by the crucified Christ of today, is encountered.

Readers may be aware of the history of debate around the interpretation of the noun "anamnesis" which is commonly translated "remembrance", as in "Do this in remembrance of me" (1 Corinthians 11,23). The literal meaning of the Greek New Testament word for anamnesis, despite its seemingly straightforward translation of "remembrance" (sometimes "recall") continues to be debated. This debate is in part driven by the parallel use of anamnesis in the Septuagint (the Greek translation of the "Old Testament"), where it is argued that the word yields a richer meaning than simply remembering or recalling an historical event. This richer, or more dynamic meaning would allow a translation of "to re-enact" or "to re-present". This ambiguity of translation may well be used, perhaps unconsciously, to support either a Roman Catholic view of the "Mass", with its emphasis on the "real presence" (of Christ) and therefore understanding anamnesis as a "re-presentation" or "re-enactment", or by the Protestant Free Church tradition to support the more usual meaning of "remembrance" in English. It is perhaps more profitable to move away from the translation debate and ask how the "words of institution" might be reinterpreted in ways which indicate what it means to be a disciple of Jesus in a contemporary setting. What does it mean to remember, recall, re-present, re-enact Christ? Is it sufficient to pass over such momentous words by understanding them simply as a means of recollection, meditation, or personal spiritual enrichment? I think not.

If such scriptural stories and their counterparts in the history of Christian experience are presented only in the language and images of the Bible, or of theology, they can, in a contemporary setting, become suffocating containers; the truth within them is trapped and stifled in ancient thought-forms and can become relegated to the realm of religious stuff-and-nonsense. It is not a case of ditching or changing the language and images (though this may be necessary or helpful in some cases) but rather of discovering a contemporary framework in which these truths can breathe more easily and which will complement the time-honoured language of religion.

At what point, does the religious experience of the Spirit converge with a developmental psychology and in what way might the ensuing complementarity overcome, or at least minimise, the above mentioned problems of misunderstanding or scathing rejection? The underlying reality of what Christians describe as the Spirit lends itself to a particularly helpful and creative complementarity. The psychodynamic aspect of this complementarity is "introjection", a concept we have already begun to look at. Expressed in a slightly different way, the psychodynamic concept of introjection sheds light on the psychological processes underlying religious experience, particularly the work of the Spirit in a believer's life. Such a complementary understanding of Spirit does nothing to degrade religious experience or to lessen the awe and wonder that human life can be so intimately and integratively linked to an experience of God. Indeed it seems to me that the picture of faith experience which many Christians term "receiving the Spirit", is not only made more credible by removing it from the realm of magical intervention (which on occasions sometimes sounds like a violation) but is more full of wonder, since it speaks of a Holy Presence who gently but powerfully (and more often than not gradually) does what God does best – self-expresses within human lives and relationships. It is noteworthy that the New Testament itself offers two contrasting ways of how the bereaved and grieving disciples received the Spirit for the first time. Acts (attributed to Luke) tells of an awesome experience, which took place after the Ascension, on the Jewish day of Pentecost:

> "And suddenly from heaven there came a sound like the rush of a violent wind, and it filled the entire house where they were sitting. Divided tongues, as of fire, appeared among them, and a tongue rested on each of them. All of them were filled with the Holy Spirit and began to speak in other languages, as the Spirit gave them ability." [Acts 2,2f]

The account of the giving of the Spirit in the Fourth Gospel could hardly be more different; here the event takes place on the eve of Easter Day, thus stressing the integration, not only of the death and resurrection of Jesus but also the giving of his gift of the Holy Spirit to them. Equally astonishing is the manner in which this gift is bestowed:

> "...he breathed on them and said to them, "Receive the Holy Spirit...""
> [John 20,22]

Those who compiled the New Testament saw fit to bequeath these two contrasting versions of this significant experience, reminding any who wish to understand that an encounter with holiness cannot be restricted to one particular place and time or to the manner of the experience.

Religious writers sometimes use the term "sanctification" to describe the change which takes place in a believer's life as a result of the "indwelling" of Christ. John Wesley, the theological force behind the 18th century renewal movement which after Wesley's death, became the Methodist Church, saw sanctification as a necessary and inevitable consequence of "justification". Sanctification (the process of becoming holy) is the outward change stemming from the inward experience of justification – a fundamental shift in relationship between the believer and God. The two experiences are not considered by Wesley as chronologically separate; he treats them individually only because one precedes the other *theologically*.

Although the terms *justification* and *sanctification* are theological jargon providing a meaningful psychodynamic framework for them helps us to see that such spiritual experiences find a place within all human experience; far from being pious nonsense, they are religious examples of what is common-place within human interaction. It may be spiteful fantasy to suggest that the lady down the road bears an uncanny likeness to the dog she dotes on but who would deny that a child not only inherits parental features but imitates and soon enough incorporates parental attitudes and habits? These attitudes and habits may, of course, be life-enhancing or belittling but at this point I wish to do no more than indicate the readily accepted *process* by which these things happen.

An experience of the Spirit as a life-enhancing encounter with Holiness finds meaning within the wider experience of human beings and with all human relationships. If such an experience is authentic – intrinsically linked to Being itself – it does not constitute a "take over", an intrusion or a violation, any more than this would happen if a person imbues the (life-enhancing) spirit of another human being. What is introjected gradually becomes part of the person. Initially there may be a conscious "aping" of the other but once this experience is chewed over and digested it becomes integral; they make it their own.

In this chapter, focusing on a central, powerful doctrine of religious faith, I have been critical of particular theologies, claims and interpretations, associated with the Spirit. To leave the matter there might suggest that I am advocating, or implying, a taming or restraining view of this central doctrine, That is not the case. Whatever the differences of opinion surrounding an understanding of the Spirit, all will be agreed that what is required is a healthy, mature view. I have already begun to suggest indicators of this in chapters 6 and 7 in the discussion on splitting, projection and the counterbalance of a movement towards integration, or in Kleinian terms, a movement from the *"schizoid/paranoid position"* to the *"depressive position"*. In what ways does closer consideration of this complementarity offer further signs of such health and maturity?

When I first introduced the ideas of James Mann into the theme of this book, I had no intention of allowing his four-fold *universal conflict situations* to drive my search for convergence and complementarity. I will continue to resist any attempt to do so, with Mann's proposals, or any other model, since that would compromise my aim all along to be led by what offers itself naturally and concurrently in the two areas of this study. However, it is a tribute to the economy and insight of Mann's framework, that I find myself naturally picking up a fourth of his (four) points: "passivity versus activity". In some ways this is the most difficult of Mann's "situations" to understand, at least initially, since the richness of its meaning is implicit in the title, rather than obvious, as with the other three. It is best that Mann speaks for himself at this point:

> The activity-passivity conflict relates to the degree of felt inner freedom, or lack of it, to pursue one's wishes or needs or aims with appropriate aggressiveness; or whether one chooses or feels compelled to wait for and expect others to gratify one's needs and wishes and aims. [Mann, 1973, p. 28]

The recognition of the need for Mann's *activity-passivity conflict* to be resolved permeates a psychodynamic way of thinking and of working with clients. When its implications are fully realized and appreciated it is clearly a fundamental characteristic of the way in which the psychodynamic therapist seeks to relate to and help the other. It is, therefore, also integral to how people get better; how they discover or regain the dignity, pride and satisfaction of self-determination. Mann's closing words of the quotation above, express perfectly the negative alternative of this movement towards healthiness; it is a sign of being less than healthy when there is a constant expectation that others will: "gratify one's needs and wishes and aims" (*ibid.*, p 28).

In therapy the therapist holds back or resists the urge to take over, or advise the client as to the best course of action; indeed for the most part does not entertain the idea that he or she, as the therapist, "knows best". The critical point however, is not whether the therapist knows best, but the need for the client to discover for themselves what they wish to be and do. It is worth noting that John's account of the Gospel, as well as using the Greek phrase which naturally translates into English as the Holy Spirit, also favours a quite different noun, (transliterated as *Parakletos*) which is variously translated as *Comforter, Advocate, Helper, Counsellor*. The word literally means "one who is called alongside", and originates in a legal or judicial context as one who represents or pleads for the accused person.

It is not difficult to find in the religious context of Christian faith and within its sacred literature, examples of how this conflict between activity and passivity is pivotal to whether or not discipleship and growth in faith is healthy or not. In the first of Paul's letters to relatively new converts to Christian faith in Corinth, he tells them that their slowness to move from "milk" to "solids" is directly related to the unhealthy nature of their attitudes and relationships:

> I fed you with milk, not solid food, for you were not ready for solid food. Even now you are still not ready, for you are still of the flesh. For as long as there is jealousy and quarrelling among you, are you not of the flesh, and behaving according to human inclinations? [1 Corinthians 3,2f]

The translation "flesh" is clearly not intended as a contrast between that which is material and that which is spiritual, as though the two were incompatible. Rather, It would not be inappropriate to say that the difference is between healthy and unhealthy lives and living.

The Corinthian letters are readily accepted as being written by Paul and relatively early (around 50AD). However, the ubiquity of this struggle to grow into mature faith, is evidenced by its occurrence in one of the latest letters of the New Testament and one which although traditionally attributed to Paul is most likely not his work:

> "You need milk, not solid food; for everyone who lives on milk, being still an infant, is unskilled in the word of righteousness. But solid food is for the mature, for those whose faculties have been trained by practice to distinguish good from evil." [Hebrews 5,12b]

It is clear in both these examples that although being on a diet of "solids" represents a more mature faith stage, being on a diet of "milk" is not bad in itself; indeed it is absolutely required in the early stages of spiritual growth. In this sense the analogy used of weaning a new-born baby works well; being held at the mother's breast, being weaned onto solids and being spoon-fed, are necessary stages of human nutritional development. The convergence here with a psychodynamic psychology is resounding. Within therapy the positive growth towards interdependence from an unhealthy dependency, and equally and inter-relatedly, from passivity to activity, lack of mourning to appropriate mourning and lack of self-esteem to satisfactory self-esteem, often requires an initial stage of "holding" the client, when there is need for great emphasis on implicitly letting the other know and feel that they are being heard, taken seriously and valued. During this time, trust can be built and the client can begin to internalise, or introject, not so much the therapist but the process of reflection and dialogue. This process will positively affect the client intra-psychically (within one's self) as well as inter-psychically (between self and others).

It has been my own experience of working as a minister of religion that the longing to receive and the temptation to continually give answers to questions about faith and life, is compelling. I have used the term "minister of religion" purposely because it implies a sort of dispensing, or prescribing and this pattern of expectation and supply can and often has become the norm for the "church-goer". I recall preaching sermons which closed as well as included questions to the congregation, including myself. They evoked a mixed response, from "You've certainly given us something to think about this morning" (which I suspect, in itself, ranged from "Thank you for that" to "I'm not sure I found that helpful" to "I prefer it when you tell us what to believe; we need answers, not questions.") Bold presentations of faith, whether in preaching, worship, theology or daily living, which include searching questions and which allow space for creative doubt, are not to be confused with tentative, unconvincing presentations which are merely an airing of one's personal thoughts and insecurities. Those who are seeking "solids" will soon know the difference. Let me return specifically to Mann's passivity versus activity spectrum.

As a child of about seven or eight out walking with Mum, Dad and younger brother in the Peak District, I suddenly (so it seemed) found myself alone. The fear of being lost and perhaps beyond that, the less conscious fear of not being found, threw me into panic. I left the path and scrambled a short distance down a wooded slope to find the shelter of a tree. With head in hands and leaning forwards on the sturdy trunk, I prayed a simple child's prayer that I might be reunited with my family. On turning from the tree and removing my hands from my face, I instantly saw my mother coming towards me and within seconds I was trotting along the path with the rest of the family. I said nothing of the strange feeling that something special had occurred, though no one observed that special feeling, nor could they have; it was peculiar to me.

Several years before the above incident, around the age of four, I had developed a "lazy eye", or "squint". Despite many visits to the ophthalmic clinic and many patched NHS spectacles, the offending eye refused to go where it was supposed to. Although a relatively straight forward operation was offered, my mother was too anxious about complications to accept the offer and the squint, only partially helped by spectacles, remained. At the age of nineteen, I became a convert to Christian faith, the story of which is not directly relevant for this book. However, with the audacity and naivety of new found faith I began to believe that what I had come to accept as impossible might become possible – through a "miracle". After all, I'd read that faith could move mountains, so why not an eye?

Night after night I would pray for the miracle to happen and morning after morning I stood before the mirror with those same hands covering my eyes again and with utter belief that the same God who had set my feet back on the safe path would set my eyes straight. The expectation was real and so was the disappointment that followed. I shared all this with an older and wiser person of faith. I recall the setting clearly. The conversation took place sitting on a bench opposite a public telephone box. (These were the days when telephone directories resided in such boxes and one inserted a few coppers and pressed buttons labelled "A" and "B"). My wise friend told me that prayers were answered in different ways and wondered whether what I thought was medically impossible might in fact be possible. There was only one way to find out, he persisted, and that was to ring the hospital. Between us we found the required coppers and the telephone number. Alone in the box, I cannot now recall what I said, or exactly how it happened but an appointment was made and a few months later an operation was performed which straightened the eyes – at least cosmetically, for at the age of 19 it was too late to correct the binocular or 3D vision.

I have ventured to tell those two personal stories because they are living examples of the struggle between passivity and activity, in the way that Mann uses the term. I learned experientially and existentially that the God I prayed to responds in different ways at different times. I don't fully understand either of the events of which I've spoken. Both can easily be accounted for, understood, or "explained away", in observable, empirical ways. For me they were and remain "miracles". Of course such a claim requires a definition of "miracle", a discussion which is beyond the scope of this book. It will have to suffice for me to say that I think these experiences are what Jacob's calls "living illusions"; they deal with the internal world as well as the external, with the subjective as well as the objective, and because they are experiences of faith, they cannot be reached directly, or understood fully.

Jacob's use of "illusion" may be criticised since it is not the commonly understood or used one. "Illusion" would almost always refer to that which is unreal; an "optical illusion" for example, or the illusion of a magic trick. I would allow that Jacobs' usage is challenging, perhaps even provocative but it does stir one's thinking and move away from a simplistic view of faith – one which suggests that matters of ultimate concern can be accessed directly and understood entirely. His challenging use of "illusion" does risk misunderstanding but I see it in a similar way to the theological and religious use of the word "myth" which indicates a spiritual truth conveyed in story form, unlike its common or secular use which immediately says, "untrue".

It may seem that I have strayed from the subject of this chapter – the concept and experience of the Holy Spirit in Christian faith. That is not the case. In fact as the themes of these chapters have unfolded, the convergence and complementarity has intensified. It is not necessary to make connections in any contrived or forceful way. It is a question rather of recognizing the complementarity as it naturally arises and presents itself. In exploring these themes I have found that more and more falls into place.

The Holy Spirit is a term used by people of faith to describe the immediacy and experiential nature of living a religious life. The Spirit is, an *illusion*; something which enables us to talk about the mystery of Holiness, which is paradoxically, at one and the same time, transcendent and immanent. It is too easy or glib to conclude that a sign of "healthy" religion is characterised by interdependence and that conversely "unhealthy" religion is characterised by a clinging dependency. This is largely and generally true but it overlooks the point I have sought to make, especially anecdotally, that it depends where a person is in their faith development and journey. What is important to say is that healthy religion is characterized by a *process* that moves from dependency to interdependence.

I wish to pursue the above point further and in a way that clarifies this area of complementarity. One of the most influential figures in psychodynamic psychology and particularly in the "school" of *Object Relations*, is that of John Bowlby. Bowlby's work is distinctive in a number of significant ways but I will limit myself to emphasising just one of these. Bowlby contends that our need for dependency continues throughout life. The difficulty Bowlby had in asserting this is the negative connotations of the word "dependency" when used to describe adult relationships. This dilemma was addressed by Bowlby's use of the concept of "attachment" and its relation to "separation anxiety" Here is Bowlby grappling passionately with the problem:

> No parent is going to provide a secure base for his growing child unless he has an intuitive understanding of and respect for his child's attachment behaviour and treats it as the intrinsic and valuable part of human nature I believe it to be. This is where the traditional term "dependence" has had so baleful an influence. Dependency always carries with it an adverse valuation and tends to be regarded as a characteristic only of the early years and one which ought soon to be grown out of. As a result in clinical circles it has often happened that, whenever attachment behaviour is manifested during later years, its has not only been regarded as regrettable but has even been dubbed regressive. I believe that to be an appalling misjudgement. [Bowlby, 1988, p. 12]

Bowlby's reformulation of the dependency/independency relationship helps to define further the place of healthiness in "healthy religion". You will recall that Mann's definition of "passivity", in his "universal conflict situation", is: "one (who) chooses or feels compelled to wait for and expect others to gratify one's needs and wishes and aims" (Mann, 1973, p. 28).

This provides a genuine complementarity with a religious person's inappropriate, infantilized relationship with "the Spirit" (God's presence and activity in and around us); unhealthy because the relationship effectively robs the person of self-determination, dignity, motivation and the enhancement of self-esteem, which flows from venturing and taking personal responsibility. My own preference for the term "interdependence", with its criticism of an on-going dependency may seem to be exactly what Bowlby is bewailing in his insistence that dependency (in the form of a need for attachment) is a life-long need. This would be to misunderstand the paradoxical tone of the word "interdependence" which carries *both* elements of dependency and independence, or we might say, by using Bowlby's term, interdependence implies and incorporates the on-going need for attachment.

If the characteristics of an inappropriate, infantilized relationship are as I have described them, their converse highlights and draws our attention to a vital area of complementarity. The Jesus of Christian faith is not portrayed as an intrusive, controlling, autocrat but as one who leaves the other space to exercise freedom of choice and dignity to make a personal decision. He is pictured replying to the would-be disciples' question, "Where are you staying?" with an invitation: "Come and see" (John 1, 38b–39a). His preaching and teaching is characterized by the use of teasing parables, challenging the listener to think through the options for herself or himself and to make a choice: "Which of these three, do you think, was a neighbour to the man who fell into the hands of the robbers?" (Luke 10,36): "Which of the two did the will of his father?" (Matthew 21,31), or more subtly, "Let anyone who is without sin be the first to throw a stone at her". (John 8,7bf), or Jesus' words to the lame man who had sat beside the pool for 38 years: "Do you want to be made well?" (John 5,6b)

The same Jesus is likened to the "suffering servant" of Isaiah, in his gentle strength, as one

> who will not wrangle or cry aloud, nor will anyone hear his voice in the streets. He will not break a bruised reed or quench a smouldering wick until he brings justice to victory. And in his name the Gentiles will hope.
> [Matthew 12,19-21, see also Isaiah 42,1–4]

All these references indicate a man whose attitude, relationship to others and mode of communication, allowed for and encouraged "healthy religion". Mann's psychological counterpart of the above is the ability: "to pursue one's wishes or needs or aims with appropriate aggressiveness" (Mann, 1973, p. 28).

The word "aggressiveness" is used here not to denote ruthless or callous behaviour but self-regard, self-confidence and the "confidence to be humble". This is where Bowlby's emphasis of the need, throughout life, for "attachment" counters any misunderstanding that an independent (rather than dependent) relationship is one that is free of the need of the help and support of others, or, if the person professes religious faith, of God. Terms such as "attachment" and "interdependence" are therefore much more appropriate than independence. It is commonplace in my experience of counselling that part of the anxiety for some people to even get as far as the counselling room door, is the feeling of having "given in". This almost always derives from a strong "family script", or "super ego" in the patient, and is vocalised in a phrase such as, "I shouldn't really be here. My mother (or father) says I ought to be able to sort things out for myself." The speaker is frequently an adult, sometimes of mature years. This kind of remark is so common that I have developed what is almost a stock answer: "I have good news for your mother. You can tell her that you *are* going to sort things out for yourself; the difference is that rather than struggling to do that on your own, you'll be doing it here, with someone else."

The above point of the need for attachment throughout life is particularly important in attempting to understand and describe the relationship of a religious believer and the Spirit, God, Holiness, or Being Itself, The complementarity here can never be precise. Even if one does not have religious faith, it can be readily understood and accepted that a relationship of a believer with what is commonly understood by the term "God" is distinctly different from human relationships; the creature is not the creator, beings are not Being Itself. The personal theology I have presented argues fervently for a more intimate and intrinsic understanding of the relationship between God and creation but this does not prevent me from concluding that there is a profoundly significant distinction between the two. In terms of complementarity, perhaps Bowlby's conviction that there is within human relationships a persistent need and searching for "attachment", unconsciously, or indirectly, resonates with that religious dimension of relationship, in which the believer is not only interdependently related to other beings but is grounded or rooted in God; in Being Itself.

The subject of this chapter has chosen itself as the closing one that offers an illustration of complementarity. It became apparent to me, in exploring The Spirit, that all that has been so far discussed converges and discloses a natural complementarity within this theme. It is as though it all finds a resolution or a "shalom" here. The Hebrew "shalom", commonly translated "peace" carries a wider and more dynamic sense than our common use of the word "peace". It more readily embraces and integrates personal, interpersonal, social and political healthiness than "peace"; it has, we might say, a more holistic meaning.

I have focused particularly on introjection as a psychodynamic counterpart to the Spirit, for obvious reasons but as Klein points out, introjection is part of a dynamic cycle in which what is taken in is also given out (projected); the latter is not always destructive or delusional (the negative aspect of projection emphasised in this book) but can serve an essential purpose, especially in the infant:

> "The projection of good feelings and good parts of the self into the mother is essential for the infant's ability to develop good object-relations and to integrate his ego." [Klein, 1946d, p. 9]

I have also expressed how Mann's four "universal conflict Situations" based on "separation anxiety", have naturally found a place as the book has unfolded; but something else has happened: all four "situations" converge particularly in the theme of the Spirit. Although I noted Mann's "unresolved grief or delayed grief" (versus suitable grieving) in Chapter 9, when referring to the Ascension, I might justifiably have chosen it for this one, since loss (in this case, the disciples' loss of the historical person of Jesus) and a healthy mourning process, are a prerequisite for receiving, or introjecting the Spirit. "Independence versus dependence" is so interrelated to that of activity versus passivity (the chosen psychological counterpart of this chapter) that no further comment is required. How does this remaining universal conflict situation of Mann's – "adequate self-esteem versus diminished or loss of self-esteem" – fit? The pointer here is to picture the contrasting state of the disciples immediately after the brutal death of their friend and master (but before the giving and receiving of the Spirit) with their confidence, self-esteem and motivation after receiving the Spirit.

On reflection it should not be a surprise that the theme of the Spirit provides a central "sea" into which all the psychological tributaries flow. The Spirit, within Christian religion (and others) represents the empowering, enlivening, enlightening, of faith experience; it is, to borrow a phrase from Iona, the *touching place.*

Conclusion

"A conclusion", someone wisely said, "is a temporary resting place." Of course it is obvious that in the strictest sense no conclusion provides the last word on any subject. In the case of this project that is particularly so, since a main purpose in writing has been to give examples; examples of convergence and complementarity between two subjectively defined areas of psychology and religion. On grounds of personal bias alone therefore, what has been written is open to criticism. I am also aware that I might have chosen a different range of examples, or included ones which the reader considers indispensable. There are indeed aspects of religion and psychology that I was sorely tempted to explore and include in the text and which I will briefly indicate in this conclusion but on the whole it feels right to rest here.

This exploration has been for me as much about discovering an approach, a methodology, as it has been an opportunity to look at particular facets of theology and psychology. I hope others can helpfully identify with this exploration and will want to pursue it further. I have found that the approach taken has freed me from more traditional methods of examining the relationship between psychology and religion. There has been no compulsion or necessity to stick rigidly with Christian doctrines as such. Allowing convergence and complementarity to call the tune has brought to light certain themes of Christian faith and life. For this reason further legitimate examples could be quite varied and might range across personal faith, social and ethical issues, or liturgical practice. The following are just two areas which seem to me to be worthy of consideration. One of these areas is clearly doctrinal but the second is thematic with strong ethical, social and political implications.

The central doctrine of Christian faith is "The Holy Trinity" (of Father, Son and Holy Spirit). Whether it was fear or wisdom which caused me to draw back from plunging into this fascinating and contentious area, I am not sure. Although I was tempted to do so, it felt as though such a large theme deserved a book to itself. My own approach to the subject of the Trinity would be to focus on its relational nature, for whatever was consciously intended by this fourth century doctrinal formulation, it is clear, in the light of modern thought, that something powerful is being conveyed about the *intra*personal and *intra*psychic nature of God or Holiness. Those with a working knowledge of both religious doctrine and Freud's metaphysical ideas may not be unaware of the uncanny resemblance between his psychological illusion (to borrow Jacob's phrase again) of the human psyche, as *superego, ego and id* and the religious illusion of the Trinity, of *Father, Son and Holy Spirit.* What, I wonder, were the Early Church Fathers unconsciously letting us know about the dynamic nature of Being Itself and further how might this relate to the fascinating nature of human beings, who simply by using a phrase such as, "I am not myself today", indicate our intrapsychic nature? The clear implication of such common sayings is that we have a relationship within ourselves, as well as between ourselves and others.

Neither theology or psychology are what they claim to be if they cannot be applied and lived out in politics, social justice and global ethical issues, as well as in personal, family and work-place relationships. One area that suggests such strong complementarity here is the issue of responsibility. I am thinking especially of the ever-present debate, in every arena of life, about how we understand human behaviour in terms of judging and making judgements about others. Are we "hawkish" in our approach, emphasising the personal responsibility which each of us must own and having little or no time for the "excuses" of having had a deprived or abusive experience in early life? Conversely, are we "doves", emphasising understanding and empathy at the cost, supposedly, of neglecting the need to accept personal responsibility for ourselves, or in others? The Bible as a whole and not least the teaching attributed to Jesus, seems to hold both ends of this debate in creative tension, as does good practice in psychodynamic therapy. Is there then a fruitful area of convergence and complementarity to be explored here which could inform us, from a wide interdisciplinary base, on issues of crime and punishment, political agendas, as well as developing a healthy personal outlook about our neighbours, near and far?

I hope these pages have been sufficiently helpful for readers to imagine areas of complementarity which I have not dealt with, or thought of, or those which I have alluded to. In closing, there are two questions which I will attempt to address. The first is, "Does it matter?" The second is, "What does religion offer which counselling therapies cannot?"

Much of what has been presented in these pages might be described as interesting theory; and yet, even if the reader finds that to be so, a critical question needs to be addressed: "Does it matter?" What benefits are there in suggesting, or even convincingly demonstrating, that the essence of Christian faith and a psychodynamic psychology can illuminate each other when allowed to interact? If there are indeed benefits they must address the lives and relationships of real people, living in the real world and trying to make some sense of it all.

I would not be writing in the way I have without being deeply convinced that the issues raised, when Christian doctrine and psychodynamic therapy are allowed to join hands, have great practical import for how we live our everyday lives. It does matter that we have an informed, mature perspective on how we function *intra-psychically*; that is to say, that we recognise a relationship *within* ourselves, consciously and unconsciously, which impacts negatively or positively on our lives and beyond. It does matter that we explore – theoretically and in relationship – how we wish to treat ourselves and others. It does matter that we break down the slippery, contentious concept of love (and the concept of the God whom love supposedly reflects) and ask what it means in practice. It does matter whether "salvation" has more to do with understanding, acceptance and generosity of spirit, than with judgement, rescue and punishment. All these things and many more have a crucial impact on how one regards oneself; how we regard and treat others; how couples relate to each other; how we speak to and behave towards our children and what we find acceptable or unacceptable in society and in political decision making.

The attempt I have made in these pages to touch on the heart of religious faith may be woefully inadequate, highly debatable, or both but no one can doubt the need for each of us to wrestle with what really matters in this gift of life. The alternative is that we lose our moorings and lose our way. We relinquish our quest to sail the high seas, with its danger and exhilaration and end up trapped in irrelevant and stagnant back-waters. I was reminded of how tragically the institutional Church can do just this as I listened recently to a radio broadcast warning that the Church of England in the United Kingdom and beyond, is in serious danger of being torn apart. The reasons for this impending catastrophe, with which many readers will no doubt be familiar, are two-fold and are worth naming for what they are. The first is that, despite the Church of England's decision in 1992 to ordain women priests, there remain Bishops who exercise their right not to appoint a woman priest to serve in their diocese. This has left the Church bitterly divided. To give a more comprehensive and balanced view It should be noted that throughout the Free Church Tradition within the UK the ordination of women has been much more readily accepted e.g. the Congregationalist Church, since 1918; the English Presbyterian Church, in the 1950s; the Church of Scotland from 1969 and the Methodist Church, from 1974.

The second reason is whether a homosexual person, woman or man, can occupy the position of Bishop in the Church and the related question of whether homosexual people are as equally regarded as heterosexual church-goers in the life of the Church. So, the Church is to sink or swim on questions of gender and sexual orientation! For some reason a television advert comes to mind in which strange Martian-like creatures, looking down on earth, are falling about in uncontrollable laughter at the sight of inferior earthlings peeling potatoes. In our case, the tears are not of laughter but of sadness.

I believe that the dynamics and doctrines of therapy and faith are at the heart of human joy and pain, for individuals, couples, families and communities. This claim does not become any weaker or less relevant when applied to the arena of national and international politics. Both religion and therapy have, in their own right, a great deal to contribute but authentic, creative dialogue between the two will have a profoundly positive and practical influence on human relationships – at every level. When religion or therapy become distorted, small-minded and petrified within their respective traditions, the human race is deprived of vital resources.

The above claim calls for greater clarification: it is not primarily about whether religion and therapy – either individually or in creative dialogue – influence human relationships. It is about the need to recognise that the psychic and spiritual processes which therapy and religion take seriously, are intrinsically related to the success, or otherwise, of being a human being, in relationship to other human beings. It is therefore both ironic and a great sadness that many who have drifted away from, or chosen to leave, the Christian religion, have done so because they experienced it as "boring" or not relevant to "everyday life". Similarly, the much younger world of dynamic counselling can easily become enclosed and rarefied, regarding its beliefs as esoteric doctrines which none but the initiated can understand. On the contrary, as with religion, the world of therapy is directly relevant to the wider world of human relationships.

No one will need convincing that for all the joys we experience in our endeavour to live together in a peaceful and productive way, misery, heart-ache, violence and exploitation are never far away. It seems that primitive fears all too often make us defensive, which in turn leads us into conflict and confrontation, invariably with destructive outcomes. The therapist, alongside the client, seeks to understand and work with the largely unconscious processes which precipitate these destructive outcomes, allowing the client to understand and accept painful, hitherto unexpressed voices to be heard, and their pain to find a degree of resolution, so that life can be more healthy for all concerned. Religion similarly offers a health-giving resolution to life's searching questions but it does so from out of the awesome claim that it speaks on behalf of One who is Creator and Sustainer of all things; who has the power of life and death and to whom we are ultimately responsible. This prompts my final question: "What does religion offer which counselling therapies cannot?"

It would of course be quite legitimate to ask the question the other way round but I will restrict myself to the former, which will go some way towards answering the latter. My reason for seeming to prioritise religious faith in this respect is grounded in my own personal development; others will choose to answer the question of difference and priority in an alternative fashion.

Psychodynamic therapy is, on the whole, a discrete form of help in which the therapist withholds her or his personal views and experience so that the client is given maximum intellectual and emotional space to come to their own decisions. The therapist may or may not be a person of faith but if the client needs to speak of religion, faith, or spirituality, whether positively or negatively, this should be perfectly possible within the therapeutic relationship. The difference between the role of the therapist and say the Minister of Religion, or Spiritual Director (or the "Christian Counsellor") is that the latter would be expected to offer religious guidance and would in any case be making a religious "statement" by virtue of their roles.

When serving as a University Chaplain and a formal Counsellor concurrently, I recall a student, saying to me towards the end of a relatively short period of counselling: "Aren't you something religious in the University?" There may have been a case for simply answering the question directly and briefly. However, there were reasons specific to this person's struggle that led me to use the opportunity therapeutically. The student was tending to look for ready-made answers and no doubt unconsciously, magical cures for his dilemma. I had this much in mind when I said to him: "I'm wondering what sort of difference it would make to you, if I were that person?" "Well", said the student, "I'm a believer and if I thought you were, I'd be more hopeful that something was happening." to which I replied: "I think maybe you're letting me know something about how you're feeling here, in our session; that nothing seems to be happening at the moment." This comment led to a fruitful conversation about how this young person needed to find strength and confidence within himself and not to clutch at the straws of other people's opinions. During our sessions I had already gained a picture of his parents as deeply caring but anxious and overprotective, so that he had little experience of making up his own mind. The counselling sessions allowed, or encouraged, that process to begin.

Religion and religious communities, like Christian Churches, are specifically different from counselling therapy, in that they are responsible for holding in trust, celebrating and proclaiming an awesome message to those who seek and wish to hear. The message is awesome because it claims to be delivered on behalf of God and in

Christian tradition, particularly through the person of Jesus Christ. Whatever words are used, the message cannot be, nor should it be, disguised, or apologised for. It can of course be accepted or rejected and debate will continue about what precisely this message is but few who take Christian faith seriously would disagree that it centres around the proclamation that the God of Christian faith, seen most clearly in Christ, is a generous, loving God, who wills the best for all people and creation. I trust it would also be generally agreed that this "message" is not necessarily or primarily communicated in words but in lives, lived out, as far as possible, in the love and by the Spirit of this God. The saying attributed to St Francis of Assisi, has a delightfully immediate way of making the point that the message needs to be lived out: "Preach the Gospel; use words if you have to."

My own commitment to the importance of therapy is evident in what I have written, and I have not tried to hide my faith commitment. The central message in Christian faith and in other faiths, of a God of love, is not and cannot be confined to religion, if as the Bible says, "The Spirit blows where it chooses…" (John 3. 8a.). However, religion has an honoured and high responsibility for communicating this message. Perhaps some people find a secular equivalent to that which faith can give but from a faith perspective, this is done explicitly, humbly and confidently by those entrusted with religious tradition. This is the tenor of a book I have already quoted from with appreciation:

> Psalm 103 begins and ends with the call to "bless the LORD", which is to acknowledge that of all the gods on offer it is the LORD alone who is God and who is the source of life and blessing. It ends with a call to the whole universe to give the LORD the recognition which is his due. In fact, the psalm begins and ends in much the same way as the Lord's Prayer begins and ends, and in its first and last words – "Bless the LORD, my soul" – those who sing or pray the psalm are invited to make that acknowledgement their own as the basis of their living, thinking and acting. [Dawes, 2006, p. 8]

Although for reasons implicitly stated in this book, I find myself in my later life, barely involved in organized religion, I remain profoundly convinced that people need to hear the lived out pronouncement that despite much to the contrary, God is, and God is love, and love is generous and renewing; that life and the universe are essentially good; that as God's expression of love, we and all creation can, as a matter of faith, live within the lightness of Grace and in the confidence that we are enfolded in love. Communicating these "mysteries" of faith is not the task of therapy but so much of what therapy seeks to do, is implicit in and deeply integrated with these mysteries. What a crying shame if the two cannot recognise their complementarity and be co-workers in doing what each is intended to.

Bibliography

Ahmad, M. T. (1998). *Revelation, Rationality, Knowledge and Truth*. New Delhi: Islam International Publications Ltd.

Bettleheim, B. (1975). *The Uses of Enchantment*. London: Thames and Hudson. [Reprinted London: Penguin Books, 1991.]

Bonhoeffer, D. (1959). *The Cost of Discipleship*. London: SCM. [Reprinted London: SCM, 1964.]

Bowlby, J. (1988). *A Secure Base: Clinical Applications of Attachment Theory*. London: Routledge. [Reprinted London: Routledge, 1997.]

Braungardt, J. (1999). *Freud on Religion*, In: ch.1. para 6, *An Outline of the development of Freud's Critique of Religion*. Essay, online: braungardt.com.

www.braungardt.com/Essays/Freud's%20view%20of%20Religion.htm#_Toc532416977

Briggs Myers, I., with Myers, P. B. (1980). *Gifts Differing*. Palo Alto; CA: Consulting Psychologists Press, Inc. [Reprinted Palo Alto; CA: Consulting Psychologists Press, 1990.]

Brueggemann, W. (1997). *Theology of the Old Testament*. Minneapolis; MN: Fortress Press.

Casement, P. (1985). *On Learning from the Patient*. London: Tavistock Publications. [Reprinted London: Routledge, 1995.]

Collins Concise Dictionary. (1982). Glasgow: HarperCollins. [Reprinted fourth ed. Glasgow: HarperCollins, 1999.]

Cross, F. L. (Ed.). (1958). *Oxford Dictionary of the Christian Church*. Oxford: Oxford University Press. [Reprinted (with corrections) 1966.]

Davies, M. (1990a). *Literary Criticism*. In: R.J.Coggins & J.L.Houlden (Eds.), *A Dictionary of Biblilcal Interpretation* (pp. 402–405). London: SCM.

Davies, M. (1990b). *Reader-Response Criticism*. In: R.J.Coggins & J.L.Houlden (Eds.), *A Dictionary of Biblilcal Interpretation* (pp. 578-580). London: SCM.

Dawes, S. B. (2006). *Let us bless the Lord: rediscovering the Old Testament through Psalm 103*. Peterborough: Inspire.

de Board, R. (1978). *The Psychoanalysis of Organizations: A Psychoanalytic Approach* to Behaviour in Groups and Organizations. London: Tavistock. [Reprinted London: Routledge, 1995.]

Dodd, C. H. (1961). *The Parables of the Kingdom*. London: Fontana Books. [Reprinted London: Fontana, 1963.]

Dominian, J. (1998). *One Like Us*. London: Darton, Longman & Todd.

Ferguson, R. (1988). *Chasing the Wild Goose*. London: Fount Paperbacks. [Reprinted London: Fount Paperbacks, 1989.]

Ford, D. F. (2003). *God in the University*. Presented as a paper at an ecumenical consultation for university chaplains.

Fowler, J. W. (1981). *Stages of Faith: The Psychology of Human Development and the Quest for Meaning*. London: Harper Collins. [Reprinted Fortress Press, 1991.]

Freud, S. (1930). *Discontent in Civilization. S.E.XXI*. In: J. Braungardt, *Freud on Religion, An Outline of the Development of Freud's Critique of Religion* (ch.1.para14.). (1999). Essay, online:braungardt.com
www.braungardt.com/Essays/Freud's%20view%20of%20Relig ion.htm#_Toc532416977

Gates, J. A. (1960). *The Life and Thought of Kierkegaard for everyman*. London: Hodder and Stoughton.

Gomez, L. (1997). *An Introduction to Object Relations*. London: Free Association Books.

Hunter, A. M. (1960). *Interpreting the Parables*. London: SCM. [Second edition London: SCM, 1964.]

Hymns and Psalms. (1983). London: Methodist Publishing House. [Reprinted London: Methodist Publishing House, 1984.]

Iser, W. (1978). *The Act of Reading*. Maryland: The Johns Hopkins University.

Jacobs, M. (1993). *Living Illusions: A Psychology of Belief*. London: SPCK.

James, W. (1902). *The Varieties of Religious Experience*. London: Penguin.

James, W. (1904). *What Pragmatism Means*. In: *Essays in Pragmatism* (pp.141-158). New York: Hafner, The Free Press, 1954.

Jeremias, J. (1963). *The Parables of Jesus*. London: SCM.

Jung, C. G. (1928). *Contributions to Analytical Psychology*. London: K. Paul, Trench, Trübner.

Jung, C. G. (1938). *Psychology and Religion*. London: Yale University Press.

Keating, C. (1987). *Who we are is how we pray*. Mystic; CT: Twenty-Third Publications. [Reprinted Mystic; CT: Twenty-Third Publications, 1989.]

Keck, L. E. (1996). Video presentation in *Disciple* training course, *Becoming Disciples through Bible Study*. Peterborough: Methodist Publishing House, in association with Abingdon Press.

Klein, J. (1995). *Doubts and Certainties in the Practice of Psychotherapy*. London: Karnac Books.

Klein, M. (1946a). Notes on Some Schizoid Mechanisms. In: *Envy and Gratitude and Other Works* (p. 2). London: Hogarth Press.

Klein, M. (1946b.). Notes on Some Schizoid Mechanisms. In: *Envy and Gratitude and Other Works* (p. 7). London: Hogarth Press.

Klein, M. (1946c.). Notes on Some Schizoid Mechanisms. In: *Envy and Gratitude and Other Works* (p. 8.f). London: Hogarth Press.

Klein, M. (1946d.). Notes on Some Schizoid Mechanisms. In: *Envy and Gratitude and Other Works* (p. 9). London: Hogarth Press.

Klein, M. (1946e). Notes on Some Schizoid Mechanisms. In: *Envy and Gratitude and Other Works* (p. 16). London: Hogarth Press.

Klein, M. (1950). On the Criteria for the Termination of a Psycho-analysis. In: *Envy and Gratitude and Other Works* (p. 45). London: Hogarth Press.

Klein, M. (1952a). Some Theoretical Conclusions Regarding the Emotional Life of the Infant. In: *Envy and Gratitude and Other Works* (p. 66. fn 1). London: Hogarth Press.

Klein, M. (1952b). Some Theoretical Conclusions Regarding The Emotional Life of the Infant. In: *Envy and Gratitude and Other Works* (p. 80). London: Hogarth Press.

Levenson, J. (1988). *Creation and the Persistence of Evil–The Jewish Drama of Divine Omnipotence*. London: Harper & Row.

Mann, J. (1973). *Time-Limited Psychotherapy*. London: Harvard University Press.

Macquarie, J. (1966). *Principles of Christian Theology*. London: SCM.

Molnos, A. (1995). *A Question of Time*. London: Karnac Books.

Otto, R. (1923).*The Idea of the Holy*. Oxford: Oxford University [Harmondsworth: Pelican Books, 1959.]

Pines, M. (1983). Psychoanalysis and Group Analysis. *International Journal of Group Psychotherapy, 33*(2): 155-170.

Phillips, A. (2005). *Standing up to God*. London: SPCK.

Proner, B. (January 22nd1997). Course lecture: *Principles of Jungian Psychology: Transference*. London.

Pruyser, P. W. (1964). Anxiety, Guilt, and Shame in the Atonement. In: H.N. Malony and B. Spilka (Eds.). *Religion in Psychodynamic Perspective: The Contributions of Paul W. Pruyser* (p. 111f). Oxford: Oxford University Press, 1991.

Pruyser, P. W. (1971). A Psychological View of Religion in the 1970s. In: H.N. Malony and B. Spilka (Eds.), *Religion in Psychodynamic Perspective: The Contributions of Paul W. Pruyser* (p. 25f). Oxford: Oxford University Press, 1991.

Pruyser, P. W. (1977a). The Seamy Side of Current Religious Beliefs. In: H.N. Malony and B. Spilka (Eds.). *Religion in Psychodynamic Perspective: The Contributions of Paul W. Pruyser* (p. 49). Oxford: Oxford University Press, 1991.

Pruyser, P. W. (1977b). The Seamy Side of Current Religious Beliefs. In: H.N. Malony and B. Spilka (Eds.), *Religion in Psychodynamic Perspective: The Contributions of Paul W. Pruyser* (p. 50). Oxford: Oxford University Press., 1991.

Pruyser, P. W. (1977c). The Seamy Side of Current Religious Beliefs. In: H.N. Malony and B. Spilka (Eds.), *Religion in Psychodynamic Perspective: The Contributions of Paul W. Pruyser* (p. 51). Oxford: Oxford University Press, 1991.

Pruyser, P. W. (1978). Narcissism in Contemporary Religion. In: H.N. Malony and B. Spilka (Eds.), *Religion in Psychodynamic Perspective: The Contributions of Paul W. Pruyser* (p. 68.). Oxford: Oxford University Press, 1991.

Pruyser, P. W. (1984). Religion in the Psychiatric Hospital: A Reassessment. In: H.N. Malony and B. Spilka (Eds.), *Religion in Psychodynamic Perspective: The Contributions of Paul W. Pruyser* (p. 96f). Oxford: Oxford University Press, 1991.

Richardson, A. (1957). *A Theological Word Book of the Bible*. London: SCM. [Reprinted London: SCM, 1962.]

Robinson, J. A. T. (1963). *Honest to God*. London: SCM. [Reprinted London: SCM, 1974.]

Rosenblatt, L. (1938). *Literature as Exploration*. New York: Appleton Century. [Reprinted New York: Appleton-Century, 1968. New York: Noble and Noble, 1976 and 1983. New York: Modern Language Association, 1995.]

Rycroft, C. (1985). *Psychoanalysis and Beyond*. Chicago: The University of Chicago Press. [Reprinted London: Hogarth Press, 1995.]

Symington, Neville. (1993). *Narcissism A New Theory*. London: Karnac Books. [Reprinted London: Karnac Books, 1998.]

Tersteegen, G. (1697-1769). In: R. Otto, R, *The Idea of the Holy*. (p. 39). Harmondsworth: Pelican, 1917. [Harmondsworth: Pelican Books, 1959.]

The Compact Oxford English Dictionary of Current English. Oxford: Oxford University Press, 2005. [3rd Revised edition.]

The Penguin Dictionary of Quotations. Harmondsworth: Penguin Books, 1960. [Reprinted Harmondworth: Pelican Books, 1972.]

The Times Newspaper. (2000). 1DDWED, edition August 2000, p. 23.

Thorne, B. (1991). *Behold the Man*. London: Darton, Longman & Todd.

Tillich, P. (1949). *The Shaking of the Foundations*. London: SCM. [Published Harmondsworth: Pelican Books, 1962.]

Williamson, M. (1992). *A Return To Love: Reflections on the Principles of A Course in Miracles*, from Chapter 7, Section 3, London: Harper Collins.

Winnicott, D. W. (1958) *The Capacity to be Alone*. In: *The Maturational Processes and the Facilitating Environment* (pp.29-36). London: Karnac, 1984. [Reprinted London: Karnac, 1990.]

Winnicott, D. W. (1971). *Playing and Reality*. London: Tavistock/ Routledge. [Reprinted London: Routledge, 1994.]

Index